STAND FOR SOMETHING

THE BATTLE FOR AMERICA'S SOUL

by
JOHN KASICH

WARNER BOOKS

NEW YORK   BOSTON

Warner Books
Hachette Book Group USA
237 Park Avenue
New York, NY 10169

Visit our Web site at www.HachetteBookGroupUSA.com

Printed in the United States of America

Originally published in hardcover by Warner Books.

First Trade Edition: May 2007
10 9 8 7 6 5 4 3 2 1

Warner Books and the "W" logo are trademarks of Time Warner Inc. or an affiliated company. Used under license by Hachette Book Group USA, which is not affiliated with Time Warner Inc.

Library of Congress Cataloging-in-Publication Data

Kasich, John.
    Stand for something : the battle for America's soul / John Kasich.— 1st ed.
        p. cm.
    Includes index.
    "FOX television commentator John Kasich issues a wake-up call to America to reset its moral compass." —Provided by the publisher.
    ISBN-13: 978-0-446-57841-7
    ISBN-10: 0-446-57841-X
  1. United States—Moral conditions. 2. Social action—United States. I. Title.
    HN90.M6K37 2006
    306.0973—dc22   2005033499

Book design by Charles Sutherland

ISBN-13: 978-0-446-69602-9 (pbk.)
ISBN-10: 0-446-69602-1 (pbk.)

To Karen, Emma, and Reese:

Because of you, I know the real meaning of love—

and because of you I know I must stand for something.

ACKNOWLEDGMENTS

This book would not have happened without Dan Paisner. He pushed, probed, and prodded to refine and focus my thoughts and ideas. He is the reason my words are captured on the written page. He has my great respect and friendship.

It was Jenny Bent who always believed that I had something valuable to say. Her confidence in me resulted in this book being written. She is truly a special person.

John Silbersack's unique ability to give a fresh perspective allowed this project to be driven forward in some very important areas. He is truly a great guy.

Rick Wolff is the guy who got me (not always easy) from our very first meeting. He took a chance on me and made many invaluable suggestions that improved this book. He has a wonderful way about him, and I hope our friendship will deepen.

Jai Chabria dedicated many of his free hours to this book. His insight, combined with his intelligence, added real value to this project. Everyone should have such a friend.

To my dear wife. You have a brilliant mind and you always close the argument.

Don Thibaut and I have worked together as friends and colleagues for thirty years. Most of our efforts have been successful. I believe this is no exception.

Ron Hartman is a friend and an advisor. His encouragement and observations made a valuable contribution.

Scott Hatch has been a valuable teammate, constantly pushing to get the best out of me. I think he did it again.

John Marucco's candor and knowledge greatly enhanced my efforts as I wrote about business in America.

Wilber James and Mark Kvamme have been my two most important shepherds as I left the government and entered the real world. Their coaching has made a deep impact on my views.

The Reverend Ted Smith has had a great and powerful impact on shaping my faith. Thank you.

John Kasich
December 2005

CONTENTS

STAND

FOR

SOMETHING

"Faith is the substance of things hoped for, the evidence of things not seen."

New Testament, St. Paul, in Hebrews 11:1

1

TAKING THE LEAD

"Hope is definitely not the same thing as optimism. It is not the conviction that something will turn out well, but the certainty that something makes sense, regardless of how it turns out."

Václav Havel

I don't know about you, but I'm troubled by a lot of what I see and hear in America's heartland. Every morning, it seems, I open the newspaper and read about some new scandal or outrage that sets me reeling. Government officials on the take. Public school teachers on the prowl. Professional athletes on the juice. Organized religion on the decline. Traditional nuclear families on the wane. And on and on. Even more troubling, it seems as though we can no longer trust what we read in the newspaper, or take in on the network or cable news programs, because the deceit and corruption have lately reached to the very institutions charged with watchdogging the public interest.

Of course, it doesn't stop at our institutions. It reaches into the very heart of our communities—the folks next door who sometimes appear wired in ways that have nothing to do with the fundamental values with which most of us were raised. Indeed, as I put the finishing touches to these pages, I'm struggling to make sense out of the latest piece of bad behavior to surface in America's backyard. And it's not just America's backyard; it's mine; it took place in a small town less than an hour from the small town where I grew up. Perhaps by the time you read this it will have blown over, but I have a feeling this one will linger in our national conscience for a good long while.

Here's what happened: A Tee-ball coach in Uniontown, Pennsylvania, was charged with offering one of his eight-year-old players $25 to hit a teammate in the face with a baseball in hopes that the targeted player—a mildly retarded autistic child—would be hurt badly enough to have to leave the game. See, in Uniontown as elsewhere, all Tee-ballers who show up for their team's games must play at least three innings, and the boy's coach thought this put his team at some kind of disadvantage. At first he thought it might be a good idea not to tell the player the time and place of the team's first playoff game, but when that didn't work he allegedly hit upon this plan to put the kid out of commission.

And the story gets worse. The coach's "assassin" missed his target on the first throw and merely hit the kid in the groin, but the boy's unsuspecting mother encouraged her son to shake it off and go right back onto the field, at which point a second ball hit him on the side of his face and ear, drawing blood and sending him to the sidelines. When I came across this headline, in June 2005, it struck me as just about the most unconscionable human act I could imagine—pure evil!—and yet upon reflection I feared it was emblematic of the win-at-all-costs, anything-goes mind-set that seems to have taken hold across this great land.

My goodness, our checks and balances are out of whack in this country, and our priorities so far out of line, that I sometimes have difficulty recognizing the world I'm living in. (Do you?) I set these thoughts to paper and catch myself wondering when halfhearted apologies started amounting to consequences; when law-abiding, God-fearing people began convincing themselves that shortcuts were the path to decency; and, when folks we'd always cast as role models started living *down* to their roles. Did I miss a memo? Was there a mass conference call, during which everyone agreed to toss aside traits like accountability and responsibility in favor of the attitude that justifies almost any action? Lord knows, I must have overlooked *something*, and at times I wonder where to look for the virtue I'm certain resides deep within us all. Like most people I know, I grew up believing that our principles were like currency, and that doing the right thing was the default option programmed into our hard drives, but these days those principles have so little to do with the heat and haste of our American way of life that you'd be hard-pressed to spot them at all in the stories behind each day's scandalous headlines.

When did this happen? And, more to the point, what can we do about it? Well, I have some ideas, and they're basic, and I mean to spend some time on them here. They reach back to this country's roots, on the theory that you've got to approach each problem at its foundation. Consider: America is a special place because of our Founders' vision. They believed that a nation could be built on the back of self-governance, that making laws didn't necessarily give us the solutions that free markets and conscience-driven individuals would also provide. They believed in the limits of government as much as they did in the power of government. And they believed that a free market economy and a limited government would be supported by our shared Judeo-Christian ethics to provide a fundamental sense of duty and conscience to all American citizens. Indeed, our moral foundation continues to flow from the shared values that have been passed down for generations, and these values are simple, straightforward, and widely held: honesty, integrity, personal responsibility, faith, humility, accountability, compassion, forgiveness. They're a part of us, whether or not we want to cop to them. What's wrong with America is that on a societal level we have swung away from these fundamental values in a kind of mass crisis of conscience—it's like a virus!—but it is up to each of us to change the tone and tenor of the country, to set right the moral pendulum in our own lives, and to swing that pendulum back in a more positive, more hopeful direction.

It *is* like a virus, and I'm afraid it's spreading. A mechanic is treated rudely and unprofessionally by a telephone agent representing one of his local utilities. Unable to receive satisfaction or even simple courtesy in the exchange, he gets off the phone in a surly mood, and finds that he is short-tempered with the next customer to appear in his garage. There's a cloud darkening his normally sunny disposition, and this next customer is unfortunately on the receiving end of it—and, also unfortunately, that next customer happens to be an emergency room physician's assistant at the local hospital, and the ill temper rubs off on him as well. And so it goes, spreading through our neighborhoods like a contagion.

Right now, the cultural indicators are stacked against us. Just look at the number of broken families—in your own neighborhood and across our country. Look at the sex and violence on television, and in our popular music, and in the video games that have become so much a part of our children's lives. Look at the number of corporate leaders under investigation, indictment, or conviction. Look at the suspect recruiting practices of college coaches, or the unbridled arrogance of professional athletes—on the field, in the locker room, and in their home communities. Look at the disturbing trend of politicians who genuinely hate each other because they wear different uniforms or hold opposing views. Look at the alarming rate of child abductions and domestic violence. Look at a system of public education that simply isn't working. Look at our disaffected student population, desperate for guidance and attention. Look at all these things and know that they exist because of a lack of leadership. That's what it comes down to, leadership, and once again it's basic. For the most part, our leaders have not been standing up for America or sounding any kind of alarm. Heck, most of them haven't been standing up at all, and this right here is the problem. For too long now, the folks who move and shake this country have been content to play the hands they've been dealt, instead of shuffling the cards and pulling for a better draw. The time has come and long gone for our leaders to rise and matter, to take a stand . . . for *something*.

IT'S ON US

Realize, it's not only our most visible leaders, our elected officials, who are failing us. The failure runs across the board. Yes, we tend to lead from the top down, but we live and grow from the bottom up, so it's not just on our senators and congressmen. It's not just on our governors. It's not just on our president, or his administration. It's not just on our favorite movie stars and rock singers and flavor-of-the-month fashion designers. It's also on us. It's on our mechanics and mailmen and teachers and middle managers. It's on our friends and neighbors.

It's on me.

It's on you.

This right here is what it comes down to. This right here is the bottom line of our societal decline. We can point fingers and lay blame and rail against our fading moral values and our rising tolerance for celebrity indiscretions, but we've got to look in the mirror and figure our own role in the mess. We've got to take some responsibility, to be honest with ourselves and consider whether we've done a single blessed thing to stand against the tides of indifference and insensitivity that have lately washed over American shores.

We are, all of us, greater than the sum of our parts. Or, at least, we all have the *potential* to be greater than the sum of our parts. In my case those parts can be traced directly to my mother and father. And that's where my potential lies as well. Truth be told, that's how it is for many of us. We draw a line from the men and women we've become to the men and women our parents tried to be, to the hopes they held out for us that first moment they cradled us in their arms. There's no denying that line. It's written all over us. Absolutely, we can trace everything about our present lives to the lives that shaped us, to the people who loved us and raised us, to the communities that held us close and kept us near. Without question, the most important gifts that my mother and father gave to me throughout my growing up were the values that came with their love and attention—the richest inheritance any parent can bequeath to a child, wouldn't you agree? Most of us have been the *intended* beneficiaries of similar gifts. (What we've each chosen to do with those gifts is a whole other muddle.) In one way or another, they're the same values parents have been trying to hand down to their children for generations, and the same values to which I alluded earlier. Honesty. Integrity. Personal responsibility. Faith. Humility. Accountability.

Being a good friend and neighbor.

Believing in ourselves.

Believing in something bigger than ourselves.

Leaving the world a better place for our being here.

Trusting in our fellow man.

I don't mean to repeat myself or to beat a dead horse but I believe in all of these values, and a few more besides. I *own* them. And I've come to realize that they're all I've got. They're what I'm made of and who I am. And the thing of it is, I know in my bones that there are millions of Americans just like me. We've all got our own core values, our own hard-won belief systems, our own ties to family and community, our own sense of right and wrong. And yet despite all of this common, value-laden ground, we live in a time of profound societal drift. We send ourselves careening into our busy lives and lose sight of our foundation. These values are like a great, welling natural resource—regrettably, one that has gone largely untapped in recent years, by too many of us. All around the country, and in our subset communities, we seem to have inched away from these core values, and the cynics among us will tell us we'll inch further still.

WHY LEGACY MATTERS

Look around and you'll see what I mean, and while you're at it take a good long look in the mirror. Let's face it, too many of us embrace these core values in theory alone, because when the gun goes off and the race begins we've seen how easy it is to shed these values to lighten our moral load. In the mad scramble to get and keep ahead we invariably forget what it truly means to succeed, to matter, to make a difference. We play every day like we're in the Super Bowl, like every decision, every action, every twist and turn will be all. But none of that matters. Well, strike that. It *all* matters, but it matters in a cumulative way, not in a big-play way, if you get the distinction. It matters in what we leave behind, in the legacy we manage to build on the backs of those decisions and actions and twists and turns. What matters is what my daughters are going to say about me after I'm gone, what they're going to tell their grandchildren—not how much money I made or how many elections I won or how many deals I helped to close. All these things matter, too, don't get me wrong, but at the end of the race they don't seem to matter most of all, and it's the *most of all* that I'm after here. It's the *most of all* that defines us.

I fall into the same traps as most everybody else. I'm not here to suggest that I have all the answers—only to ask the right questions, and to keep asking the right questions until we begin to push each other to some kind of shared awareness. I'm so far from perfect I sometimes need a map to find it, but I'm on it. I'm trying. I'm doing everything I can, as opposed to as little as I can get away with, and this is all the difference. The effort. The doing. The taking care. Too often, I find, folks resign themselves to whatever they think fate has in store for them. They make mistakes, as we all do, but they really drop the ball when they choose to live with those mistakes, or to compound them with other missteps. I worry that our young people are looking over their shoulders at the world around and figuring there's no profit in rocking the boat or shaking things up or taking any kind of stand—and it's this very complacency that threatens our shared moral fiber.

Here's just one example: I work with students in a leadership program at Ohio State, and they often wonder what the point is in making any kind of extra effort or going any kind of extra mile. They get to thinking the odds are stacked so long against them that there's no point in reaching out to make any kind of difference, and this was brought home to me one day in class when one of the students suggested that all Martin Luther King, Jr., ever got for his troubles was a bullet. Another student chimed in with a story about her aunt, who railed against unfair business practices at her place of work and in return received a pink slip. Others checked in with their own tales of frustration and woe, and somewhere in the middle of the debate the mood of the room seemed to be that there was no profit in fighting our big institutions. Now, I hear this type of thinking enough times and I begin to realize how powerless our young people feel. They're stymied, with no real idea how to move up and out and forward. Clearly, there's a hopelessness out there that I'm afraid is insidious and I'm worried that if we don't stand against it, and soon, we'll be headed for even more desperate times.

And so I try to impress on these students—our future, the seed corn of our society—that nothing good was ever accomplished with complacency. I remind them that change doesn't just *hap-*

pen. I listen about their aunt who might have lost her job and help them to recast that proud woman as a role model, a real champion for change. I tell them about Martin Luther King and what he was able to build from his strength and vision. I help them find the points of connection, from how this great man was raised to how he lived, and to recognize that it's the same line that reaches all the way back to the Bible. That's what was so brilliant about Martin Luther King. He captured the notion that if we stand on principle—God's principle, that all men are created equal and that we will not respond with violence against those who are violent—then the righteousness of our cause will ultimately prevail.

I don't wish to be the voice of doom here, and I certainly don't mean to suggest that Western civilization is lost and hopeless. Not at all. There's an awful lot that's right and good about the way we live and work. It's like there's a hole in the dam, and if we don't tend to it the dam is going to burst. Think once again of our young people and you'll get what I mean. Think of the images and impulses that have been raining down on them for as long as they can remember. Think of the world we've made for them and the one they're about to sustain. Somehow, they've gotten the message that it's okay for professional athletes to climb into the stands and pummel unruly fans, for gangster rappers to denigrate women and celebrate violence in the name of sales, and for the bottom line to measure the sum total of how we live. It's no wonder they're jaded, and confused. You would be, too, if all you knew was that Paris Hilton is rich and famous for no good reason but the confluence of birth and reality television, and that baseball player Rafael Furcal is allowed to drive under the influence without immediate punishment because his team is in a pennant race and a judge allows himself to be persuaded in the court of public opinion to let his sentencing slide until the end of the season, and that politicians can purposefully mislead their constituents on the staggering public debt that threatens our nation's financial security and still be reelected.

THE (AGONIZING) THRILL OF VICTORY

Like I said, our priorities are out of whack, and we need look no further than the hopeful exceptions to this truth to see how far we've actually strayed. You'll find as you read along that I sometimes look to the world of sports to help me make a point—probably because there's no richer, more illustrative arena for stories involving good guys and bad guys. It's all about winning and losing, and in that context it's easy to spot the tension between bending or breaking the rules and upholding them. It's clear-cut. In sports, the space between honor and dishonor is sometimes measured in fractions of a second, or a couple of inches, and as cultural indicators go there's no better gauge on who we are, what we do, how we live, and why it all matters. Take golf. Goodness, what a beautiful game. In golf, you can find all kinds of useful life lessons. Every golfer lives and dies by the same set of rules, I don't care if you're Tiger Woods or a weekend duffer on your local public course. And yet within those rules there's some wiggle room, and that's where we get ourselves into trouble.

Davis Love III offered a compelling lesson when he was competing for our country in the Ryder Cup. For a golfer, that's the closest thing to heaven. There he was, battling it out on the 18th hole, even up, and what did he do? Well, as bad luck would have it, he drove the ball into the rough, and this is where some of that wiggle room entered into it. In golf, there are rules that allow you to reposition yourself or your ball by a club length in certain circumstances, and here Davis Love III was legitimately allowed to stretch out and hit the ball with his feet positioned on a drainage pipe and thereby move his ball from the heavy rough to the lighter rough, giving him an easier shot. But he didn't do it. Understand, he was playing for the honor of his country. It was the 18th hole. The Cup was on the line. The match was tied. Each stroke was huge. But Davis Love III chose not to stretch out and take advantage of the rule because he thought it violated the spirit of sportsmanship. It would have given him an edge he didn't feel he deserved, so he played the ball where it lay and hoped for the best. (How about *that*!) As it happened, Love made par and tied the hole, and I looked on at home and thought, Man, isn't this something! To give up an edge just because it wasn't sporting and to still hold on under tremendous pressure, with your entire country pulling for you . . . it was a selfless, noble act. Wonderful. Pure. Maybe even a little bit heroic. And it made a giant impression on me.

Another golf story. Tom Lehman is one of the best golfers on the tour, and a Christian man. In June 1996, playing the U.S. Open at the Oakland Hills Country Club, he found himself in the final round of play, walking the 17th fairway with his good friend Steve Jones, another Christian man. Both were among the leaders. It was the second consecutive year that Lehman played in the final pair at the U.S. Open, itself a significant accomplishment, and he would go on to play in the finals in the next two Opens as well, and here he famously cited Bible verses about strength and character and purpose to the man he was battling for the tournament. Imagine: You're Steve Jones, chasing your first major, and you're just back from a dirt-bike injury that cost you three years on the tour; your tournament is on the line, and your opponent is lifting you up with a verse from Joshua 1:9:

"Be strong and courageous. Do not be discouraged or afraid, for the Lord your God will be with you wherever you go."

Pretty amazing, right? And yet that's precisely what Tom Lehman was doing, sharing these inspiring words. So what did *he* do? Well, he hit his ball into the bunker, while Steve Jones, the man on the receiving end of Lehman's good counsel, drove the green and captured the championship. Think for a moment how incredible that must have been, for Tom Lehman to share those powerful words with Steve Jones, just as Moses once shared them with Joshua. At the time, I would have probably been saying a silent prayer that Steve Jones would drive his ball into the drink, but I've tried to learn from Tom Lehman on this one, because he was able to put the competition into perspective. He was able to communicate by his actions that sportsmanship matters, that fellowship matters, that character matters. Really, that's what it comes down to.

And the story didn't end there, because a couple months later, Jones found himself paired with another active Christian, Paul Stankowski, in the final round at the Kapalua International, and on the 17th tee he started quoting Joshua 1:9 to *his* opponent. (I'm telling you, this virus concept is catching, don't you think?) Fittingly, this time it was Stankowski who was lifted to victory, and he later told a reporter it was "a neat deal, that someone under the gun, trying to beat my brains in, is trying to offer me courage."

A neat deal? Man oh man, you better believe it! And here's the capper. Later that same year, Lehman found himself battling it out for the British Open and this time found the strength and courage in himself to take the title, and I'd like to think he deserved the victory—but of course he'd have probably said that his actions at Oakland Hills had nothing to do with his British Open win, even as it spoke volumes about the man and the kind of competitor he was.

I know it pains most duffers to admit it, but there's more to life than golf—and there's more to sports than just winning. Just ask Steve Jones, the guy who took Tom Lehman's generosity and generously passed it on. "I've never prayed to win," Jones said after his victory. "Tom Lehman hasn't either. I think that's the totally wrong attitude. What Christians should be praying for is to glorify God, no matter what happens."

Amen.

One final golf story—this one from my old congressional district, at Ohio's Mount Gilead High School. Adam Van Houten, a sixteen-year-old sophomore, was in position to win a Division II state golf championship when he realized that his playing partner had reported an incorrect score for Van Houten on the 10th hole on the second day of play. Van Houten usually kept his unofficial score on a slip of paper, but there were high winds on this second day of play and the paper was carried off by a breeze at some midpoint in the round. Without his own scorecard as corroboration, Van Houten signed his partner's scorecard, and it wasn't until later, as he was replaying the round in his mind, that he realized he had shot a 6 on the 10th hole instead of the 5 his partner had noted, giving him a 74 for the round instead of the 75 he deserved. Even so, the 75 would have combined with his 70 from the opening round to place him comfortably in the lead, so it appeared the "honest" mistake would have no impact on the championship.

But Van Houten knew he had to report the correct score, even though by doing so he would be disqualified. "I knew I was going to win," he said later, "and I knew what would happen when they found out. But I never considered not telling them. I could never live with myself."

He went to his coach with his dilemma, and together they approached the on-site representatives of the Ohio High School Athletic Association. As expected, Van Houten was disqualified, although the tournament officials offered high praise for his integrity. "As a teacher and a coach for twenty years, I've never seen a situation remotely close to anyone showing this much character," Van Houten's coach later told reporters. "He knew he was going to lose the state championship. It makes me so proud he's on my golf team. I'll never look at the kid the same way again."

The kicker here is that Van Houten would have won the tournament by six strokes—even without the extra stroke saved on his partner's scorecard. He could have kept quiet and still known in good conscience that he didn't gain any advantage by the error. *And no one would have known.* But that wasn't how this kid was cut.

It all comes back to character, don't you think? It's key. In my first book, *Courage Is Contagious*, I celebrated the under-the-radar accomplishments of ordinary people doing extraordinary things to change the face of America, and here I might suggest that character is contagious as well. After all, it's not just our *negatives* that can spread like a virus, but we can catch each other's virtues as well. Let's hope character is contagious, because we would all do well to catch a good dose of it and pass it on—like Tom Lehman to Steve Jones to Paul Stankowski. Sadly, it strikes us as extraordinary when we come across a person of character these days, but it should be the norm, and I don't want to lower the bar so much that we start celebrating what is merely expected of us.

The problem with character is that we've allowed our popular culture to redefine it for us. What's held out as an ideal for one generation is rejected by the next, and those of us looking to toe some sort of line are left scratching our heads and wondering how those lines keep getting redrawn. But I choose to believe that character—*true* character—is written on our souls. It's timeless. It's in our bones. How else to explain how we know what we know? The Bible tells us not to kill, and not to covet our neighbor's wife, and not to take the Lord's name in vain, but there's a whole lot more that we know without being told. The difference between right and wrong, justice and injustice, honor and dishonor, virtue and vice. We don't need to be told these things, or to read it in the Good Book, to know them for ourselves, instinctively, and yet more and more I see otherwise well-intentioned folks looking the other way from what they know to be right and good and true.

A STUDY IN CHARACTER

On a societal level, it sometimes seems we don't have the first idea how to stem the flow of bad behavior. Government regulators climb all over each other to install tougher rules and regulations to curb the greed and malevolence of some of our corporate leaders, but rules can never be a substitute for character. That's a line I stole from former Federal Reserve Chairman Alan Greenspan, who cautioned that excessive regulation risks ancillary damage by discouraging risk taking. He's right, it will. We can't legislate character any more than we can require a creative spirit of entrepreneurship among our business leaders. You've either got it, or you don't, and no law or regulation is going to help you on this one. We can't fix corporate America or cure the ills in any other aspect of our society simply by drafting a new set of rules to tell us what we should already know for ourselves. We *know* the difference between ethical behavior and unethical behavior, even as there are some among us who seem intent on blurring the lines. We *know* we shouldn't be skimming monies from our employees' pension accounts, or subverting shareholder interests for short-term personal gain. We *know* not to inject ourselves with banned substances to gain a competitive advantage on the playing field. We *know* that our fiduciary responsibilities are inviolate and that to shrink from them is unconscionable. We *know* that our commitment to marriage and family should supersede any selfish impulses in pursuit of some other happiness. And yet we stray from what we know, from time to time—not all the time, mind you, but often enough to suggest an alarming trend.

Most alarming of all, perhaps, is what has happened in our political arena. For me, after nine terms in Congress and a stalled bid for the 2000 Republican presidential nomination, this hits especially close to home. What troubles me here is the way we've developed an us-versus-them mentality in government. There no longer appears to be any room for healthy debate or considered differences of opinion. I don't know whether to pin this one on talk radio, or twenty-four-hour cable news channels, or bloggers passing themselves off as political pundits, or on the politicians themselves. Or maybe it's because of our disturbingly short national attention span. Whatever it is, we have poisoned our political system to where it's all about what uniform you're wearing. Perhaps this trend can be traced to a lack of leadership that might encourage dialogue across party lines. What we lack are statesmen who put country first and party second, leaders who stand on principle, who can reach agreement when possible and fight with dignity and compassion when necessary. And yet we've been reduced to thinking that everything the opposing party does is suspect and that everything our own party does is honorable, and we have lost the ability to build consensus or to seek middle ground.

In Washington today, it's all about finding and maintaining some type of edge and forging alliances that cut only along party lines—and the same holds true in politics at the state level. It's all black-and-white, with no shades of gray. And, lately, it's become personal. Good people allow themselves to be chased from office because they don't want the opposition to come gunning for them, and at the other end there's little incentive for men and women of character to seek public office when doing so puts them in such a vitriolic line of fire.

I served in Congress for eighteen years, and I could rail against our present political system for eighteen more—and yet it's only with perspective that I have come to understand the deep-seated resentment and frustration that people feel toward their elected officials, and to recognize that a good deal of it is justified. Frankly, I share some of that frustration. I shudder when Democrats and Republicans attempt to deal with the coming generational crises that threaten American stability by adhering to their own party platforms. I cringe when my good friend checks into the hospital on an outpatient basis for a partial knee replacement and is presented with a $31,000 bill, because our health care costs have run so far away from any kind of sensible economic scale that no partisan approach could ever confront the problem. And I bristle when well-read, educated people reach out to me after one of my speeches and wonder how America will survive the next four years if their presidential candidate doesn't get elected, because our campaigns have lately been painted with such broad, do-or-die strokes that even well-read, educated folks are moved to think the future of their unborn grandchildren hangs in the balance.

I can remember being in the Congress in 1994, sitting on the House floor as Pat Schroeder walked by. Pat was a liberal Democrat from Colorado whom I happened to like. I haven't seen much of her lately, but I like her, because I have regard for people who don't think the way I think. Just so you think, that's all I ask. Take a stand. I don't care what you stand for, but stand for something. Believe in it, and work toward it, and talk me into it if you can. That's how it was with Pat Schroeder and me, as it was with me and many of my Democratic colleagues throughout my political career. Remember, the Democrats were in the majority at that time, and right or wrong it was seen as somewhat unusual for politicians of different stripes to have a friendly conversation on the House floor, but that's precisely what we did. Pat had just had a hearing on one of my bills and passed it out of her committee, so we had a few things to kick around, and after we'd parted a few freshman Republicans came up to me and wondered what *that* was all about.

"How could you talk to that woman?" one of them asked.

It was as if I'd been found guilty of treason—or, at least, caught with my hand in some partisan cookie jar. I couldn't believe what I was hearing. "What's wrong with you?" I shot back. "Pat Schroeder is not the enemy. This isn't war. She's one of your colleagues."

"But she's a liberal Democrat," came the sheepish reply.

These newly minted Republican congressmen couldn't even grasp what I was trying to say to them, that's how foreign it was to their way of thinking, and I didn't fault them as much as I did the system they were about to enter. They were perhaps too green to know any better—but how to explain the veteran congressmen who felt the same way? And furthermore, how to explain that it's gotten worse, in the dozen or so years since this exchange took place?

I'll tell you another strange-bedfellows-type story, as long as we're on it. Long before he became governor, Arnold Schwarzenegger called me up toward the end of Bill Clinton's second term as president, and asked me to meet with a friend of his named Bono. He said he doubted I would have heard of this guy, even though the CD carousel in my car was filled with his music. I laughed at Arnold, but agreed to meet with Bono, even though I was always wary of so-called celebrity experts on public policy issues. Bono wanted my help on debt relief for Africa, which was a big issue for him at the time and had always been a big issue for me. So we met, and I agreed to help him, and I took Bono to Capitol Hill, where one of his greatest champions became Jesse Helms. What a coalition we put together: Chris Dodd, Pat Leahy, Jesse Helms, Rick Santorum, and myself, and many others, basically covering the waterfront on the political spectrum.

In the course of working on this issue, I helped put together a meeting with religious leaders over at the White House. I invited Pat Robertson to attend. Pat told me he had not visited the White House since Clinton became president, and I soon learned that Clinton's staff wanted to keep it that way. At one point, they actually asked me to disinvite Robertson, who had been highly critical of Clinton, to which I said, "Well, then I won't show up." The staffer went in and cautiously advised the President that Pat Robertson was scheduled to attend the meeting, and the President looked at him hopefully and said, "Do you think he might come?"

The meeting took place, and we were of all stripes: rabbis, priests, ministers, Irish rock 'n' rollers, Midwestern congressmen . . . The meeting was a success, and at the end I could see Pat Robertson and Bill Clinton yukking it up at the front of the room, and I turned to that anxious staffer and said, "Now do you believe in miracles?"

Good politics shouldn't be about *us* or *them*. It shouldn't be about winning or losing. Good politics should be about doing. If you win, that's great. If you lose, that's okay, too, as long as you've worked tirelessly for your ideas and your ideals. As long as you've done something—because, here again, the accomplishment is in the doing. It's in the effort, the taking care. Talk to a successful businessperson and he or she will tell you their version of the same thing. They'll tell you they're not searching for profits but for excellence. Build the best widget, design the best system, offer the best customer service and the profit will come. Run the tightest ship and you're less likely to spring a leak. In politics, if you're always searching for votes you're a panderer. Ultimately, you get the votes because you stand for something. In business, if you're always searching for excellence you're an industry leader and it's clear to all what it is you stand for: quality, achievement, value. Ultimately, you get the business because you've earned it.

KEEPING FAITH

Two subjects central to this discussion, of course, are religion and family, so let's make room for them here. Just so you know where I come from on these fronts, I was an altar boy as a child, a card-carrying Catholic from a small, working-class, church-abiding community. (More on this a bit later on.) It's unbelievable and unacceptable to me that the Catholic Church has not been completely accountable for the various scandals that have enveloped it. The molestation and sexual abuse charges. The duplicity. It's enough to drive a mailman's son from McKees Rocks, Pennsylvania, to question his faith—until I realize that we must separate the church from the individuals who presume to be in charge. People come and go, priests come and go, but it's the religion that matters. It's the religion that sustains us. I would never force another individual to believe what I believe, but I feel strongly that we all need to believe in something greater than ourselves, and I also maintain that once we define that something we need to invest in it wholeheartedly. Not in the people who preach it or administer it but in the belief itself.

Another thing you'll find as you read along in these pages is that I like to circle my various points to where I can bring things around and sound a resonant theme. In this case, my circling takes me back to golf—because, after all, religion is a lot like golf, don't you think? (No, I don't suppose you do, but stay with me and you'll see what I mean.) There are a whole mess of rules in most every religion, just as there are a whole mess of rules in golf. If you tee off and you hit it out of bounds, you tee off again. You take your stroke penalty and move on. But golf is not about the rules. When you sit down and talk about your latest round, you don't talk about the rules. The rules are simply taken for granted—and you abide by them, for the most part. You don't give your ball a more favorable lie. You don't grab a new ball from your golf bag to replace the one you lost in the woods without taking a stroke penalty. In any case, you aren't *meant* to do these things, although there are exceptions to even these rules. Once, I was playing with a good friend of mine who didn't take the rules as seriously as the rest of us in our foursome, so I good-naturedly called out to him and said, "Hey, you're not supposed to move your ball." To which he good-naturedly replied, "Hey, you're not supposed to be looking."

My point here is that the rules of golf are not the object of the whole enterprise. They're not what golfers dwell on. They dwell on the game itself, on the enjoyment they derive from it, the relaxation, the camaraderie, the competition, the fulfillment of a well-played round. Once again—the doing, the taking care. The same holds for religion. It's not about the *don'ts*; it's about the *dos*. It's not about the judgment; it's about the grace. It's not about the downside; it's about the upside. It's not about our faults; it's about our potential. And the great thing about religion is that it's shot through with second chances. Come clean, own up to your mistakes, resolve to do a better job the next time out, and all is forgiven. It's like a spiritual mulligan, a do-over, an opportunity to start anew.

Is it necessary for an individual to be a religious person in order to be an ethical or moral person? On an individual basis, probably not, but in a large, sprawling society I think it's essential. Anyway, that's my view. Without a calling to some higher authority, without a belief in something bigger than ourselves, we'll never figure things out. I look on the Bible as a kind of spiritual roadmap, offering a constant touchstone that can help me withstand the ebb and flow of contemporary society, pointing me in directions that ought to be intuitive. Even better, it's like a blueprint. Anybody can build a crooked house, but to do it right you need that blueprint. You need that foundation. And it's easy enough to get confused, sorting through our mass media and popular culture. We are, at bottom, a country built on the principles of Christianity and Judaism, and yet we make abundant room for Muslims, Buddhists, Hindus, and believers of every other faith. Good for us. Good for *all* of us. Whoever you are, and whatever your beliefs, you can come and live among us.

We've tightened up our borders a bit, since September 11, 2001, and in some communities our tolerance thresholds have been challenged as we attempt to coexist with our Arab friends, but America's open-door, melting-pot, inclusive approach remains essentially intact: You can build your temples here. You can enjoy our American way of life. You can buy into the same deal, same as anybody else, but for the whole lot of us to survive and thrive as a pulsing, booming society there needs to be that religious foundation, and there ought to be some uniformity within that foundation. Clearly, our Founding Fathers recognized this as well—celebrating our Judeo-Christian principles in our Constitution, in our Pledge of Allegiance, in our currency, and in virtually every significant building block of our American foundation. The Jewish and Christian religions that flow from these principles give us our shared conscience, and provide an essential bulwark for any free and dynamic society.

FAMILY TIES

As foundations go, not a one stands as strong as the American family, although recent developments suggest I should temper this one a bit to state that not a one has the *potential* to stand as strong as the American family. I think we'd all agree that there has been a steady erosion of the importance of family in our me-first, get-it-while-you-can society, and hand in hand with that erosion is a sharp increase in the national divorce rate and a steep decline in what politicians have taken to calling family values. But what are family values, after all, if not a harking back to a simpler, more innocent time, when our lives weren't so chaotic, and our choices far less likely to get us into trouble? I grew up in a time and place where it was okay for a kid to hop on his bike first thing in the morning, ride down to the schoolyard, and spend the entire day bouncing from one unplanned activity or encounter to the next, until the sun started to sink low and it was time to pedal home for dinner. And yet times have changed, and I don't think you'd find too many parents in too many communities who allow their children the same kind of autonomy. These days, our kids' lives are so heavily programmed and supervised it's a wonder they ever learn to think for themselves. It's the lament of nearly every parent I know with young children, that their family dynamic is built around short car pool rides to dance-art-music-karate-soccer-gymnastics lessons and that there never seems to be any time for anything else. No chance to just sit and talk, or think, or read. Not enough time for our children to daydream, or to amuse themselves. Sometimes it seems that parents, particularly working parents, have become so busy that they measure their success as parents by their availability to drive those dance-art-music-karate-soccer-gymnastics car pools. Fathers playing catch with sons? You can just forget about it in a great many American households, unless it's a scheduled activity, with a reminder tacked to the kitchen bulletin board, to be done in the company of dozens of other harried fathers and sons on a town field.

And what about our families wracked by divorce, or desertion, or disinterest? How can we go about fixing these broken homes when so many of us can't even manage to get it right in our intact, nuclear households? It's enough to get you to throw up your hands in despair, and yet we press on, because we are a resilient lot, and because we are steadfastly determined to get it right for the sake of our children. That next generation is always a powerful motivator. I know in my case, I started looking at the world through a different lens once I became a father. I got around to it fairly late, and when I finally did I caught myself second-guessing a lot of my decisions, and wondering how my actions might make me look to my kids. Big things and small, it's all about setting an example, and taking the lead, so I make sure to keep my seat belt on even when I'm in the driveway, and I make sure to treat people decently, even when it's one of those telemarketers who seem always to interrupt us during dinner. Don't tell your daughters one thing and do something else, I've learned, because they don't care what you say; they care what you do, and they remember what you do, and they learn from what you do. Oh, you better believe it.

Our children are the greatest equalizers in the world. They keep us honest, and striving. Or, at least, they should. I often joke that we should live our lives as if there were some sort of mommy-cam or daddy-cam jury-rigged to record our every move, so that we would at all times conduct ourselves as if we were being watched by our children, but I'll let you in on a little secret: It's no joke. I'm serious. We should live like we're being monitored, because we are. We *are* being watched. We *are* setting an example. We *are* being judged.

Lately, I catch myself wondering how much of what people say in their eulogies is actually true, and it occurs to me that we would all do well to make it our business that at least three-quarters of the nice things people say about us after we're gone should be somewhat accurate. That seems like an attainable goal—and a lofty objective.

I think in this context of a guy like Stephen Ambrose, the great historian who fell from public esteem at the tail end of his notable career. Remember him? He wrote books about Custer and Crazy Horse and World War II. Prize-winning, best-selling, critically acclaimed histories that cast him as a true chronicler of the American experience. I've got his books stacked all the way to my ceiling, I thought they were just marvelous, and then I picked up the paper one day and read about how he'd been charged with plagiarizing his material. I picked up another paper the next day and there were new charges of same, and my first thought was, What am I going to do with all these books? And it wasn't just Ambrose. For a while there, a number of prominent writers and historians were made to deflect similar allegations, including Doris Kearns Goodwin—a Harvard Ph.D. whose incisive accounts of the Kennedys and the Roosevelts and the Red Sox put her on the best-seller list, and whose apparent failure to footnote certain passages put her on the defensive.

In Goodwin's case, she seemed to salvage a good deal of her reputation by copping to the charges against her in what ways she could. She called herself sloppy and lazy. She admitted to paraphrasing certain material, and neglecting to credit some of her sources, and readers and fellow scholars seemed to want to cut her some slack. Ambrose wasn't so lucky. He died of lung cancer soon after all those charges were brought against him, and his reputation was perhaps permanently stained. There was a prominent obituary upon his death, and it was a beautiful tribute except for one sentence, and as I read it I wondered, How much would his family have given to take out that one sentence? What would Ambrose himself have given? Indeed, how much would all of these people pay to turn back the clock and undo their mistakes and missteps and miscalculations? To reclaim whatever it was that their parents or grandparents tried to teach them? To uphold the values that at one time or another had upheld them?

MAKING A DIFFERENCE

I went into politics for one basic reason: to change the world. It sounds like a line, and in some respects I suppose it is, but it's also the God's honest truth. I didn't go into it to become a wheel in some well-oiled party machine. The Republican Party was my vehicle, not my master. That's not what drove me. What drove me then and what continues to drive me now are ideas. Issues and ideas. Doing the right thing. Being heard. Making a difference. I was elected to the Congress of the United States at the age of thirty, and many of the people I grew up with didn't know what to make of me because politics was such a tarnished profession. In fact, I went to one of my high school reunions at some point during my tenure in Congress, and this one guy walked up to me and said, "Hey, Johnny, I voted for you as most likely to succeed. What the hell happened?"

It was, I thought at the time, a good question, and I ask my own version of same as I consider the world we've all made for our children. *What the hell happened?* We've increased our federal deficit by hundreds of billions of dollars, adding to the trillions of our national debt. We've blown an opportunity to take some of our surpluses and put them to work saving some of our biggest, most essential social programs. We've let Social Security deteriorate to where more eighteen-year-olds believe they stand a better chance of seeing a UFO in their lifetime than a Social Security check. We've seen health care costs spiral out of control, and unconscionable legal fees scare honest, hardworking folks from starting or sustaining their own businesses. It's downright depressing if we don't look at the bigger picture, and the bigger picture is this: What goes around comes around. For every valley, there's a peak. Everything's on a pendulum, folks, and it's only a matter of time before fate and fortune swing back in our favor. We need look no further than our recent history to remind ourselves that such swings are the nature of the American beast. Everything old is new again. Our slumps will replace themselves with hot streaks—provided we grab hold and do what we can to swing the pendulum back in a more positive direction.

Right now, as I stated at the outset, I believe we're in a leadership slump. That's just how it is, but it won't be this way forever. We'll elect and appoint new leaders and they will rise to the occasion. People say there will never be another Franklin Roosevelt, but there will be another Franklin Roosevelt. There are only a few folks still around who felt the full effects of the Great Depression, but a whole lot of us were alive to take in some of the ripple effects. You might think your 401(k) took a hit when the bubble burst on all those Internet stocks, but that was nothing up against the Depression. People jumping out of buildings. People unable to get their money out of their banks. People looking desperation in the eye and not liking what came back in the reflection. I can never shake the image of my father and his brother—my Uncle George, who later became a guidance counselor and who had a tremendous positive influence on thousands of kids—going to school in clothes fashioned from old flour sacks, that's how hard the Depression shook our family tree. And yet Franklin Roosevelt got up on that stage at his first Inaugural and delivered a line that's as appropriate today as it was back then: "There's nothing to fear but fear itself." *That* was leadership.

Roosevelt knitted together perfect strangers who all became part of a single American family. You've heard your fathers and your grandfathers tell you about going to the store with no money in their pockets and putting their purchases on a tab, but there was rarely any tab. These store owners carried their long-time customers because it was the right thing to do, and because Franklin Roosevelt empowered and emboldened them to do so. Because he made us feel we were all a part of the same family. Working together. Struggling together. Succeeding together.

Franklin Roosevelt led us through the Depression, and then he took us through a world war with the same unflagging principles. In 1939, when Hitler invaded Poland, 95 percent of the American people said it was none of our business. Heck, there were even people inside the Roosevelt administration who suggested we make a deal with Hitler. Can you imagine what the world would look like today had we made a deal with Hitler? It's unthinkable, and yet we came through that Depression and that world war and we emerged as the most powerful nation in the history of the world. *That's* leadership. That's courage, and vision. And that's inspiring people to a higher purpose.

Back to sports again, for just a beat. I can't write about that time in American history without invoking Jesse Owens, the dazzling runner. There's a monument to him outside Ohio Stadium, and he is always very much on the minds of the folks in my hometown, so he stands front and center as I write this. You want to talk about leadership? This was a guy who stood up to Adolf Hitler in those Olympic games in Berlin, and showed the world what it meant to be free. He didn't pump his fist in the air, or gyrate his hips, or showboat like some of today's athletes. He just went out and got it done, and in so doing he made a powerful statement that shook the world.

Now, consider what passes for leadership in some parts of the world today. The spiritual head of Hamas, the radical Palestinian group, sends a woman (the mother of two children) on a suicide bombing mission in a busy Israeli square. She wears a belt filled with dynamite, and also with bullets and screws so that when she exploded she could kill more people. Not soldiers, but innocent men and women. And children. This made headlines the same week we celebrated Martin Luther King's birthday in this country, and I had a hard time considering the one without the other. The violence against the nonviolence. The swing of the pendulum that will inevitably swing back our way once more. King wrote, "No law of man that does not square with the law of God is moral." He wrote this from a Birmingham jail cell, and in the same missive he vowed not to return violence with violence, and when he was released from jail he marched. His supporters complained that they were being beaten and gassed, but still he marched, and in so doing he offered the kind of inspirational leadership and determination that ultimately connected with our shared sense of decency and justice. And all across the country, in white suburban America, people took up King's cause. We demanded change on the strength of his leadership.

And, always, I look at my hero. Ronald Reagan. He was unbelievable, and one of a kind. Character. Principle. Walked the lonely road. Challenged Americans to make their own difference. Recall that when he first came into office he was succeeding a president who told Americans to beat the gas crisis by riding their bicycles to work, to beat the oil shortage by wearing a sweater. Reagan took one look around and essentially said, "What are you guys, nuts?" Interest rates were out of control. Inflation was out of control. The Cold War against the Russians was at its zenith. So what did he do? He sent Jeane Kirkpatrick to the United Nations and delivered a powerful message that the rest of the world was not going to kick America around anymore. He cut marginal rates. And he took on the Soviet Union. He called them the "Evil Empire." His advisors said, "Mr. President, that's not good politics. That's not good diplomacy." And Reagan just chuckled and said it anyway.

Once, on his way to the Brandenburg Gate, Reagan's advisors were pleading with him to temper his comments. (Reagan's secretary of the treasury, James Baker, told me this story.) "When you get to the Berlin Wall," the advisors told their president, "please, remember we're in the middle of sensitive negotiations. Be careful what you say." So what did Reagan do? He strode to that gate and he took the lectern and said, "Mr. Gorbachev, tear down this wall."

Ronald Reagan didn't listen to his advisors. He didn't listen to his pollsters. He trusted his gut. And he united the whole world. Mothers and fathers who had locked themselves in their homes in fear showed up in town squares in Poland and Czechoslovakia and in the Baltic states. They stood, and lit candles. "We're not going back," they said. "We want our freedom." Reagan's words echoed through Eastern Europe, and soon enough the Berlin Wall came tumbling down and millions of people were returned to their rightful way of life, to freedom.

LIFTING FROM THE BOTTOM

That, friends, is true leadership. But we can't all be Ronald Reagan and Martin Luther King and Franklin Roosevelt. They're big shots, but it's not about the big shots; they can never be our country's heart and soul. Their actions are critical, but I think it's clear that America is moved from the bottom up. I know a guy named Albert Lexie, and for my money Albert is the heart and soul of America. He dropped out of school when he was fifteen and took up shoeshining for a living. That was his calling. Albert's a little different from the rest of us. He actually listens when he asks you how you're doing. You give him an answer. He listens. So, right there, he's different.

One Sunday afternoon, Albert was at home watching a KDKA telethon on Pittsburgh television, to benefit the children's hospital there. And, watching, he fell in love with a little girl he saw on the telethon and with the thought of how he might help her, so on Monday morning he went to his bank and withdrew every penny he had in savings. Eight hundred bucks, give or take a couple pennies. Albert Lexie took that money and went down to the hospital and gave them every last cent. Hospital administrators found out about this, and a little bit about Albert Lexie, and they reached out to him and asked him to come shine shoes at their hospital. To which Albert responded, "Look, I'm pretty busy. I can give you two days a week." Which is just what he's done—for the last twenty years. He hops a bus for the half-hour trip to the hospital, straps on his tool box, which weighs about thirty pounds. He's got all his stuff in there. His brushes, his polish, and his special "magic" sauce that gives his customers that extra shine. He goes from doctor's office to doctor's office, nurse's station to nurse's station. Spend any kind of time in that hospital on Tuesdays and Thursdays when Albert's working and you'll see doctors and nurses traipsing around without their shoes on. He's become a fixture—an oasis for folks desperate to talk, to get their minds off whatever else it is that brought them to the hospital in the first place.

He charges three bucks for a pair of shoes, and he slips that money into his right-hand pocket because that's what he lives on, but he takes his tip money and slips that into his left-hand pocket, because that's what he means to donate back to the hospital. Over the years, he's collected more than $100,000 in tip money, and he's used that money to help parents cover their bills and other attendant costs associated with their children's long-term care. He was voted Pittsburgh's "Philanthropist of the Year" in 2000, and it was about time. And, it was about leadership.

Guys like Albert Lexie are the heart and soul of this nation. They move America every bit as meaningfully as Franklin Roosevelt or Ronald Reagan. And it doesn't end there. In our communities—big and small, rich and poor—we struggle with education. The knee-jerk response is that we're not giving our public school children what it takes to meet the challenges of today, and in many schools that's unfortunately the case. Not so at the Frederick Douglass Academy, a small public school in Harlem. The school was shut down in the late 1980s due to excessive violence, but it reopened in the middle 1990s with renewed promise. It was still located across the street from a burned-out crack house, but it was now being run by folks with the vision to look past their surroundings. Now, the kids don't go to school in their Britney Spears T-shirts, or in baggy pants "sacked" halfway down to their knees. There's a dress code, and there's no wising off to the teacher. Students say, "Yes, ma'am" and "No, sir." There are no study halls or free periods or gut classes that encourage students to skate by on little effort. If you do well in trigonometry, you get kicked up to advanced trigonometry. They've got rules, and expectations, and if you mean to stay there you've got to meet them all.

And guess what? The students are thriving. They've gone from wondering where they're going to get their next meal to wondering where they're going to go to college. The first graduating class in 2001, there were 105 graduates. Out of that group, 104 went on to college. The one student who didn't go to college became a Navy SEAL. In 2002, there were 120 graduates and each and every one of them went to college. And in 2003, they were 115 for 115—netting over $5 million in scholarships. Not bad for a bunch of administrators and teachers dedicated to old-fashioned values like hard work and teamwork and discipline. Once again, for good measure, that's leadership.

Okay, so what does all of this have to do with the rest of us? We're not Jesse Owens or Davis Love III. We're not Albert Lexie or the administrators at the Frederick Douglass Academy. So what about us? Where is our shared ability to recognize and harness this type of leadership in our own communities, in ourselves? Where is our responsibility to stand tall in the face of all these low expectations? For me, the answer comes in a book written almost two thousand years ago: St. Augustine's *Confessions*. It's a tough little book, written in the fifth century, but I take it with me wherever I go. It's got a powerful message that I believe resonates here. St. Augustine maintains that each and every one of us has a special gift, and that it falls to each and every one of us to unwrap those gifts and share them with the rest of the world. I like that image a whole lot, because I look at gifts like I look at stars. Have you ever seen an ugly star? I never have. They're all just magnificent. You look through the telescope and see that some of them are red and some of them are blue. Some of them flame brightly in the night sky and some are so far off as to be nearly unrecognizable. And every last one seems just about as special and magnificent as a thing can be, but none of them are quite the same. That, to me, is a true gift. We find them in the heavens, and we find them here on earth. We find them in our friends and family, and we find them in ourselves. And, significantly, we find them in our leaders.

Now, here's what I know, as sure as I set my pen to paper: Discover your own gifts and you will give your life new meaning. Find the courage to share those gifts with the rest of us and you will give all our lives new meaning. I can't tell you what your gifts are, just as you can't pinpoint mine, but I can tell you they lie in wait. Oh, they're out there, waiting for you to come upon them and put them to good use, and it is in the putting to good use of our unique gifts that we will rediscover our health and strength as a nation. After all, we are all stars, in our own way.

We all shine uniquely. We all share the power to grow and change and reimagine the world around. Find your gift and you will find your way. Join a team. Become a part of something bigger than yourself. Throw in with all of the other stars in your community and help to form a giant constellation, built together on the back of courage and faith and determination. And, above all, leadership. Take charge. If you see something happening that sets you off, rise up and do something about it.

Stand for something.

Right now, in our post-9/11 world, Americans are standing tall in the face of people who want to destroy us. They want to destroy us just because of our way of life, and yet here at home that very way of life is threatened because we've taken it for granted. And so, yes, let's keep fighting the good fight. Let's stand brave and proud. But while we're at it let's also rediscover the moral compass we seem to have misplaced. Let's reclaim the roots and values that shaped us as children and that will someday protect our grandchildren. And let's reboot our free enterprise system, to where our thirst for success is no longer just about making money but also about the good we can do in the course of turning that profit. I'll give an example: I'm on the board of a company that makes wheelchairs. Inevitably, the profit motive drives us to be successful. It drives us so hard that our engineers have now perfected our wheelchairs so that people can do just about anything in them. Imagine that. There are thousands of wheelchair-bound people who couldn't get out of their homes who can now move about town on their own steam, thanks to this wonderful development. People are playing tennis in these wheelchairs, conducting orchestras, competing in the Boston Marathon, and performing in the Cleveland Ballet's Dancing Wheels dance troupe . . . and I look on and think this is not only a tribute to the good works of this one company but to the society in which we live.

Indeed, the American free enterprise system takes ideas and translates them into innovations that can change the whole wide world, and it falls to our leaders to keep the regulators and the lawyers and the politicians from muddying up the works. And yet underneath all of this enterprise and courage and lead-ership is that core set of values I wrote about earlier, values that give conscience to us all, and underneath these values is an undying faith. I listen to all of these extremists and activists who appear determined to beat religion from our lives, and I think to myself, These people are nuts! An America without religion, without our core set of Judeo-Christian values, is an America in chaos. We'd be lost without those values. We might lose sight of some of them, from time to time. We might rethink some of them, from time to time. We might even reject or suppress some of them, but there's no erasing them. They're a constant, and they will remain a constant. Without them, we've lost America, and so we sit tight and hold fast and wait for our friends and neighbors to grab on to what we already know.

And what we know is this: We answer to a higher power. We're accountable for our actions. And we can't change the world by relying on anybody else. It's on the Tom Lehmans and the aunt who stands in protest over conditions at her place of work. It's on us. Remember, everyone is a shepherd to someone else, whether it's your kids or your grandkids or your neighbor's kids or their grandkids. They are watching you. Life is short. Play hard and play fair. And always remember those values your par-ents taught you. Follow the rules, respect authority, treat people fairly and decently, take care of business. Do the right thing. Leave this place a little bit better because you were here. That's the way we want to be remembered. Put it all together and let it stand as three-quarters (at least!) of the sum total of what people say about you after you've gone.

SHINE A LIGHT

The book you now hold in your hands, through which you've read to these introductory remarks, is intended as a kind of beacon. A lighthouse. The values we've learned from our parents, they're like a lighthouse as well. They don't move, or change. They've been around forever and they will last forevermore. They're built on a bedrock underpinning that remains constant in a sea of change. They remind us daily that truths are intuitive, and that it's the popular culture that confuses us. If lighthouses moved with those shifting seas, think of the trouble they would cause for sailors navigating their ships in the middle of a foggy night. If we tweak our values to justify our societal drift, we're lost. If we move with the tide, we're lost. If we rethink the lessons of our lifetime on the fool notion that doing so might keep us relevant or plugged in to our popular culture, we're lost.

No question, we live in challenging times—and our ability to meet its challenges runs alongside our ability to lead. To once again embrace the simple truths that defined our growing up. To hold fast to our faith. To make a difference. To matter. To stand for something.

Let's get about it.

2

TAKING MEASURE

"The family is the first essential cell of human society."

Pope John XXIII

I grew up in a small Pennsylvania town outside Pittsburgh called McKees Rocks, the kind of place where hard work was often its own reward, and where everyone knew most everyone else.

My father was a mail carrier. My mother also worked for the post office, sorting mail. Between the two of them, and the connections they established, it sometimes seemed I couldn't cross the street without being spotted as their son. I supposed then, and know for certain now, that these points of connection were a great, good thing. If Hillary Clinton is correct to assert that it takes a village to raise a child, then McKees Rocks was certainly up to the task. God knows, it took a village to raise me. Whether they meant to or not, the good people of McKees Rocks helped to shape and define the person I would become. They encouraged me and set examples that continue to inspire me. It was an ethnic, blue-collar community, long in moral fiber and short on excuses. Regrettably, the moral fiber didn't reach to a great many of our elected and civic leaders, because as I recall the McKees Rocks of the late 1950s and early 1960s was marked by a whole lot of graft and corruption and questionable decision making, but the tone and tenor of the town was very much opposed to the pacts and tactics of politics and government.

What we lacked in creature comforts, we more than made up for in values and ethics and perseverance and doing the right thing—and on this score at least, we Kasichs were pretty darn wealthy. Indeed, we had everything we needed, and a little bit more besides. We were a churchgoing family, to the point where I used to think I'd grow up to be a priest. At ten, when I was in fourth grade, I wanted to become an altar boy, so I applied and was accepted in record time. I committed all these difficult Latin phrases to memory, and learned the services, and devoted myself fully to the task, to where the assistant pastor at one point commented that I knew the services better than he did.

One Sunday, after I'd been at it for a few years, our priest asked me to lead the church as a commentator. The commentator leads the congregation in readings and song, and folks were genuinely surprised to see such a young kid assume the role. It was my first public speaking appearance, and I haven't stopped since, although I was nearly derailed in this regard early on. I mistakenly instructed parishioners to turn to the wrong page in their hymnals, and when they didn't appear to be singing along with enough conviction I instructed the organist to stop playing so I could have a word with them from the pulpit. Naturally, I couldn't expect them to sing with conviction after I had directed them to the wrong page in their hymnals, but I didn't know that at the time. All I knew was that folks weren't singing with their customary enthusiasm, and that I had been charged to lead them.

"Sing it like you mean it," I implored.

To their great credit, the parishioners gave it their best shot, considering the circumstances, and it wasn't until the service was over that an elderly parishioner came over to tell me of my mistake. I was red in the face with embarrassment, but I share the story here for the way it illustrates how our townsfolk nurtured and even indulged their own. Of course, my critics might suggest that it also illustrates my overzealousness, and in this instance they might have a point, but I share it anyway because I've never shied from telling a good story on myself.

HOME

The McKees Rocks of my growing up was a Democratic stronghold, and my parents were committed Democrats, although my mother became a Republican later on in life. We didn't carve up our national map in red states and blue states back in those days, but if we did my hometown would have checked in looking about as blue as a high, cloudless sky. John F. Kennedy was a great big deal in our neighborhood, as I recall, and so, too, were the liberal ideals of the times. But these ideals were rooted very much in faith and family, community and common sense, and even as I grew to disagree with my parents and our friends on certain fundamental points I recognized that at bottom we were coming from the same place—and, for the most part, headed in the same direction.

Case in point: As a young teenager, I was in the habit of calling the local talk radio stations to speak my mind on various issues of personal interest, and as often as not my views tended to land on the conservative side of the spectrum. My mother was well aware of my leanings, and she often listened to these same shows, although she had no idea I was an occasional caller. One afternoon, she was downstairs in the kitchen, listening to the radio, when she heard a well-spoken young man sound off in a way she thought I might find interesting, so she set off looking for me. She hollered, "Johnny, turn on the radio!" Then she burst into her bedroom—only to find me on the upstairs phone, doing the sounding off.

Another case in point: I had a math teacher named Ed Gregga. Mr. Gregga turned out to be a tremendous, upstanding guy, but at the time I didn't think he was a very good math teacher. I actually tried to get out of his class, but eventually he and I became friends. He told me a story I've never forgotten. It seems Mr. Gregga's lifelong dream was to be the head football coach at McKees Rocks High School. He'd been an outstanding college player—an All-American at Juniata College—so he was certainly qualified for the job, and it finally came his way. He was like a kid in a candy store, he told me many years later, finally realizing a long-held goal. And he was successful. For a couple years, he did a great job with the McKees Rocks varsity, and then out of the blue he was visited by one of the town leaders, who wanted Mr. Gregga to start ordering the team's equipment and uniforms from a friend of his who owned a sporting goods store in town.

Now, Mr. Gregga was inclined to do no such thing. He ordered his sporting goods from Honus Wagner's, a competing store, and Honus Wagner's had been good to Mr. Gregga and to McKees Rocks High School. When the school was in financial trouble, the good people at Honus Wagner's carried them for a couple seasons, and Mr. Gregga wasn't about to forget it. He said as much to the town leader. He said, "Sir, I might buy my shoelaces from your friend's store, if it means that much to you, but I'm buying my helmets and shoulder pads and all that other equipment from Honus Wagner's."

The town leader said, "I'm afraid you don't understand. You're gonna buy the equipment from me, my friend, or else—"

Mr. Gregga didn't wait around to hear the *or else*. He said, "Well, then I guess I just quit." And he did. He walked away from his dream job—a job he was good at!—because he would not be pressured in this way, and because he would not turn his back on people who had not turned their backs on him.

That was McKees Rocks for you—shot through with graft and corruption and shady dealings, but at the same time filled with principled people like Mr. Gregga, people who weren't afraid to stand for something. I mean, here's a guy who gave up his dream job for something he believed in. His values meant more to him than worldly success—and to him, being head coach of the high school football team was worldly success. But he wouldn't play ball, so he had to give up his dream and redefine what it meant to be successful.

MY FATHER

Here's my father for you, in a nutshell. I was about eleven years old, and one by one my friends were being asked to play for this or that team in the local Little League. There was a massive try-out, and a series of lesser tryouts, and some sort of disbursement draft, and when it was all said and done a few of us kids had managed to fall through the cracks and not get selected at all. I was skinny, small, and too easily overlooked. Nowadays, you'd have to look long and hard to find a youth sports program that doesn't make room for all interested participants, but things were different back then. Parents weren't tuned in to buzzwords like *inclusion* and *positivity*, and *playing fair* was an oxymoron; getting "cut" was an accepted part of the deal.

In any case, I was a huge baseball fan, and like every other kid in McKees Rocks I dreamed of someday playing for the Pittsburgh Pirates, and yet there I was, missing out on my chance to play any kind of organized ball. I was a smart kid, and a decent enough ballplayer, and it took about a heartbeat for me to see what was going on. No, I wasn't one of the strongest players in town, not by a long shot, but I wasn't one of the weakest, either. Some of these other kids were getting picked for teams because their fathers were coaches, or because their fathers were friendly with the coaches, or because they knew the guy who was sponsoring the team. And yet there I was, overlooked again and again and again. Even at such a young age, I could see that life and Little League were all about connections, so I went up to my father one evening and made my frustrations known. I told him I was as good a ballplayer as Jimmy or Jeffrey or Jerry, and that he needed to go and talk to somebody and get me on a team. He knew everyone in town, I reminded him. He delivered their mail, and chatted with them on their doorsteps. Surely, I suggested, there was someone he could talk to about getting me on a team.

My father saw the situation a bit differently. He said, "Johnny, I'm not going to owe anybody anything. I'm sorry, but you're going to have to earn your way on to one of these teams."

Let me tell you, that was a tough lesson for an eleven-year-old kid, but I tried to swallow it. I wasn't mad at my father, and I don't think I begrudged him his position, but I did have a hard time understanding it. All I could see was that these other kids were playing ball and I wasn't. That was the long and short of it. My friends all had their uniforms and their team practices, while all I had was my pile of disappointment, and it got to where there wasn't even anyone around for me to have a catch with, but I kept at it. As I recall, I did a lot of tossing the ball high up into the air, over and over, or practicing up against a wall. My father would throw the ball around with me, every chance he got, and even as a kid I could tell it was tearing him up inside to see me so distraught, but he held fast to his principles. He would not go with his hand out to anyone, for anything—certainly not for something like this.

A couple weeks into the season, some kid broke his leg and I got my shot, which I guess means that in the end I got to play without my father being beholden to anybody in town, and it's a shame it had to happen as a result of someone else's misfortune even though at the time I didn't spend too much time worrying about the poor kid with the broken leg. I just grabbed my glove and raced to the field for my first practice, thrilled to finally be getting a real uniform, and the chance to play for a real team.

And no one was happier for me than my father, in part I suspect for the way it got him off the hook, but mostly because he knew what it meant to me.

I don't know that I would have handled the situation the same way if I had been in my father's shoes, but this was his principle. This was his stand. And, in the end, what did it accomplish? Well, for one very important thing, it made an impression. Here I am, a lifetime later, still telling the story. Here I am, still thinking about the lesson it carries, the values it upholds, the example it sets. I read the great Czech playwright and leader Václav Havel, who suggests that it is arrogant to believe a single righteous act *can't* change the world, and I find my own father between the lines.

"A human action becomes genuinely important when it springs from the soil of a clear-sighted awareness," Havel writes in *Disturbing the Peace*. "It is only this awareness that can breathe any greatness into an action."

Was there greatness in such a small act as this? No, probably not. Was there even a clear-sighted awareness on the part of my father, that his principles were not only *his* principles but that they might soon become mine as well? That they might set an impossible standard? Again, probably not. He was doing what he felt was right, and just, operating within his own moral code, and he expected me to shoulder my situation and move on. And that might have been that, but for the fact that his principles continue to resonate, all these years later.

MY MOTHER

Here's my mother for you: One afternoon, she took me to a fair at the schoolyard. Some kid had brought a pony to the school and was offering rides for 10 cents apiece, and I stood dutifully on line with my mother and waited my turn. The kid who was running the rides wasn't much older than me, and he looked down on his luck. His clothes were a little too torn and tattered, his face a little too smeared with sweat and effort, his demeanor a little too hangdog to suggest prosperity. There was even something *off* about one of his eyes, it left him looking one way when he meant to look another, and I may have only been six or seven years old but all these things registered. As excited as I was to ride the pony, that's how sad I was at the sight of this kid.

Sure enough, my turn came and my mother handed the boy a dollar for the ride. That was a lot of money to us, back then. I don't mean to portray us as impoverished, but as I wrote at the outset we didn't have a whole lot, and we certainly didn't have enough to pay a dollar for a pony ride. That was a real extravagance. I tugged on her dress and said as much to my mother. "It's only ten cents for the ride," I whispered, when she stooped to hear what was on my mind.

"Quiet now, Johnny," she said, in a whisper of her own. "Can't you see he needs it more than we do?"

And he did.

My mother was a keen and compassionate observer of the world. She took things in, like no one else I've ever known. Nothing escaped her attention, or her concern, and it had me thinking she was always one step ahead of everyone else. There could be an edge to her, and you wouldn't want to be on the opposing side of an argument at a PTA meeting or family discussion, particularly on a substantive matter that involved real principles and ethics. Her greatest concern was for her own children, for helping us to find and embrace whatever joys might come our way, and her extra efforts in this regard were everywhere apparent. When the Pirates won the 1960 World Series in stirring fashion, for one memorable example, my mother knew what it meant to me to take the bus downtown to be a part of the celebration. I was all of eight years old, and we muscled our way through the crowd and even managed to get Bill Mazeroski's autograph on a baseball, creating a memory I didn't think I had any right to seek. That trip to downtown Pittsburgh that evening was hectic and chaotic, but it was a trip my mother was only too happy to make for her baseball-mad son. It didn't mean a thing to her, but it meant the world to me—and that, to my mother, was everything.

They were simple people, my parents. Good, honest, hardworking, God-fearing people. Call-it-like-you-see-it, tell-it-like-it-is-type people. My father was easygoing, got along with everybody, and he just loved his job like crazy. It fit his personality. He was charming, and somewhat gregarious, which in many ways ran counter to his own backstory. His parents had struggled mightily. My grandfather was a coal miner in western Pennsylvania; he eventually died of black lung disease. As an immigrant, his employers often took advantage of him, and he was so beaten down by his situation he didn't feel he could make a stand. They were dirt poor, my grandparents, and I guess that kind of upbringing instilled in my father a clear sense of station. In his mind, success was reaching to the next rung on the economic ladder. It was lifting yourself up and out and onto something better. Success was owning a car, or keeping ahead of your debt. It was raising a family, and going to church, and being a good neighbor and living a decent, purposeful life. My mother shared this view. Her family was also extremely poor, and her parents barely spoke English. And yet they never lost sight of their principles and believed deeply that having compassion for others was one of life's great treasures.

Together, upon these mighty foundations, my parents made a fine home for their three children, and filled it with object lessons on faith and decency, common sense and compassion, integrity and hard work. I don't know that they would have ever put it in just these terms, but they dedicated themselves to improving their children's future and creating a great American legacy.

There was no stigma to being a mailman's son, back in McKees Rocks, the way there might be today in so many parts of the country. Everyone was the son of a mailman, the son of a mill worker, the son of a policeman. Delivering the mail was honorable work, and at the end of a long day that was all that counted. There were no shortcuts to success in my parents' estimation, no back doors to opportunity. Hard work and character were key.

GREAT EXPECTATIONS

I grew up with great compassion for the underdog, perhaps because I came from a family of underdogs. Nothing was ever handed to us; we lived and grew in the reaching. There's a wonderful maxim—"To whom much is given, much is expected"—only my parents seemed to want to turn the message around: "to whom nothing is given, everything is expected." My parents set the bar high, and I aimed to clear it. When I was old enough, I borrowed a page from my mother and stood tall for what I felt was right. There was a race riot in our school. There were precious few blacks among our student body, but there was enough tension to get a full-fledged riot going, and I took the microphone at a school board meeting and berated the community for not doing enough to ease that tension. I didn't think about it; I just stood and said my piece. And do you know what? Folks listened. I was barely seventeen years old, confronting several hundred adults in a real crisis situation, shining what I hoped was a positive, hopeful light, and I somehow got to the heart of the matter and stilled the crowd. Why? Because I'd seen my mother argue with anybody about anything—as long as she believed in it. Because it seemed to me to be the right thing to do. Because it was in my bones. Because it needed doing.

It was always a given that we kids would go to college. That was another measure of success, to my parents, to ensure that their children had more opportunities than they had themselves. I can still remember driving to my Aunt Betty's house on Sundays, past the Cathedral of Learning at the University of Pittsburgh, and my father leaning over the front seat of the car and saying, "Johnny, is that where you're going to college?"

The message was clear: If I remembered where I came from, and focused on where I was headed, anything was possible; dream big dreams and they just might wind up turning true on you.

When it came time for me to move on I didn't stray all that far. Lewis and Clark went clear across the country to realize their dreams; I went just 180 miles to the west to Ohio State University to discover mine.

There were 48,000 students at Ohio State in 1970 and I found myself in a dormitory that was twenty-three floors high and filled with eighteen-year-old freshmen and women. We lived in a common suite that was about the size of a couple elevator cabs. They stuffed sixteen of us in this tiny little suite. I swear, whoever designed it wanted to flunk us all out. To make matters worse (or, better, depending on your perspective), right next door was a duplicate tower, also twenty-three floors high, also filled with eighteen-year-old freshmen and women. Let me tell you, those dormitories were like two giant Petri dishes for every imaginable type of human behavior—and some unimaginable types as well. If there was trouble to be made, these young dormitory residents were on it, and under it, and all over it. In downtown Columbus, the locals used to refer to these towers as Sodom and Gomorrah, and back then there were hundreds of undergraduates determined to justify the name.

Naturally, in that kind of setting, there are countless rules put in place to keep order and sanity. One of the big rules in those high-rise dorms was that you couldn't open the windows. I guess the "men" and "women" who came before me liked to throw things like water balloons from those upper floors, and I guess, too, that this practice was generally frowned upon. I was in my new suite with my fifteen new roommates for about fifteen minutes before every single one of these rules was broken, and the thing of it is not one of them was broken by me. I was terrified of being away from home at this point, and terrified of stepping out of line, so I went by the book.

GO BUCKEYES!

Ohio State University, like most big institutions, relies on its rules in order to keep thrumming—and this was especially so during my tenure, as American college campuses became a flashpoint for protest, unrest, and social change. Somehow, second or third week of school, I allowed myself to get so worked up about all these rules that I wanted to talk them through with someone in charge—and it seemed to me the only place to get a meaningful hearing was in the office of the university president. That's how I thought back in those days, and I guess that's how I still operate, reaching to the very top in order to get to the bottom of things. And so, fueled by a series of now forgotten frustrations, I reached. I worked my way through layer and layer of Buckeye bureaucracy, all the way up to the president, Novice Fawcett, and it just so happened that Dr. Fawcett had a secretary who did a pretty good job running interference. I called to ask for a meeting, and she put me off. I called again, and she put me off again. I must have called about fifteen times before she finally said, "You're driving me crazy, young man." To which, of course, I could only reply, "Ma'am, I mean no disrespect, but I'm going to keep calling your office until you put me on the president's calendar." I was polite and courteous and all those good things my parents had taught me to be, but I was also persistent. I even said something about coming down with my sleeping bag and camping outside the president's office door, if that was what it took to get a meeting with him. I was nice enough about it, but I pressed the point.

Well, this last must have struck some kind of chord. That, or she finally realized what she was up against. Anyway, she said,

"I'll tell you what. Forget the sleeping bag. You just come on over tomorrow morning and we'll see if we can't get you in to see him."

And that's just what I did. I put on my best blue jeans and my best blue jean shirt and my best (and only!) necktie, and I stuffed my hair up under my hat and walked over to see the president. Novice Fawcett was a very big, tall guy. About six foot five, in his socks. I'd seen him before—welcoming new students from the podium at Freshman Orientation, striding purposefully from one administration building to the next, looking positively presidential in his head shot on the front page of *The Lantern*, the student newspaper, but he cut an even more striking figure up close. He had a beautiful office. Big desk. Big wooden chairs. Big tables. Fancy artwork decorating the walls. Very impressive. Really, it was almost overwhelming, that's how imposing it was, and the combination of this giant, formidable man, with this giant, formidable name, sitting behind his giant, formidable desk made quite an impression on me, and as I sat and lodged my complaint and offered my observations I couldn't shake thinking that I had stepped into the headquarters of accomplishment and power.

It was, if memory serves, an awesome meeting—or, at least, it seemed as such from where I sat. The president listened patiently and with what I took to be great interest. When I was finished, he spun around in his big wooden chair and said, "Young man, what are your plans?"

I wasn't sure at first if he meant my plans regarding this particular matter, or my plans in general, and chose to assume the latter. "I'm not sure, sir," I said. "As you know, I've only been in school here about a month, so I'm still undecided, but I've got to tell you, as I look around this office, I'm thinking this could be the job for me. What, exactly, does a university president do?"

I was genuinely interested in what this man did for a living and how I might consider doing it myself. At that time in my life, I was hungry for insight into other people's choices, other people's careers—and I still am, I should mention. Anyway, I thought a big, impressive office would be just the thing, especially with the services of a secretary who so fiercely guarded my appointments calendar.

Novice Fawcett seemed only too happy to talk about his career to a straightforward young gun like me. He told me about his academic responsibilities, and his fund-raising responsibilities, and his responsibilities with the school's trustees and administrators. It all sounded very interesting and important. At some point, he mentioned that he was flying to Washington the next afternoon for a meeting with the President of the United States. It was October 1970, and Dr. Fawcett had been the only president of a major college or university to have endorsed Richard Nixon during the 1968 presidential campaign, and he was finally being invited to the White House for a brief meeting as a kind of public thank-you for his support.

In October 1970, this struck me as about the most impressive thing I had ever heard, and I said as much. It was a big deal to the entire Ohio State community, I'm sure, but it was an even bigger deal to me. When you're eighteen years old, and full of yourself and confident in your abilities, you tend to speak your mind a lot more freely than you might as a card-carrying adult. I even had the temerity to ask in on the adventure. I said, "Well, sir, I've got a number of things I would like to talk to him about as well. Do you think I could go with you, as a kind of student ambassador?"

The president considered this for about a millisecond, and then without a trace of humor or kindness responded flatly: "No."

He wasn't nasty about it, but he could clearly see no reason why one of his students would even ask such a thing and why he should have to consider it.

"Well, how about this?" I continued, not willing to be put off. "How about if I went back to my dorm and wrote a letter and you could give it to President Nixon for me?"

Dr. Fawcett thought for a while and probably figured there was no good reason to deny my quite reasonable request. He had never met me before, and apparently wasn't in the habit of receiving students in his office, but he shrugged his shoulders and said, "I guess I could do that."

In retrospect, I realize this man could have easily tossed my letter in the trash and never followed through on his courier pledge and I never would have known the difference, but I took his consent to deliver my letter as tantamount to receiving an audience with the President of the United States. All of a sudden, I could not have cared a whit about the issues that had brought me to this office in the first place. All of a sudden, this unlikely opportunity to bend the President's ear was all I could think about. I raced back to my room and wrote a letter—a letter that I firmly believed would be read by the President. When I ran out of things to say, I signed the note and offered to consult with the President at length on any matters, if he should require my insight. "P.S.," I wrote, "if you'd like to discuss this letter further, please don't hesitate to contact me. I'll make myself available. I'm a college student. I've got time. I'll come to you."

That was decent of me—wasn't it?—to offer to go down to Washington to see the President on his own turf? I mean, if I was being *really* presumptuous, I would have suggested *he* drop by to see *me* next time he was on campus.

MR. KASICH GOES TO WASHINGTON

A couple weeks later, I opened my mailbox and found a return letter from the Office of the President of the United States, on official White House stationery. My heart raced, and I ripped into that envelope without a thought for saving it for posterity. Sure enough, President Nixon had written me back, telling me he found my letter intriguing and thoughtful and allowing that, indeed, he would like it very much if I could come to the White House to discuss these relevant matters further. He said that someone from his office would be in touch with me in the weeks ahead to make arrangements. I set the letter down feeling like I was on top of the world. His staff must have seized on my letter as a photo opportunity of some kind, a chance to show American voters that President Nixon took pains to keep in touch with America's young people on the issues of the day, but all I could think at the time was that I had engaged the most powerful man on the planet, in such a way that he wanted to meet me and hear more.

I thought, How great is this?

First thing I did was head for the dormitory phone to call home. My mother answered on the first ring. "Mom," I said, "I'm going to need an airline ticket. I'm going to have to fly to Washington to meet with the President of the United States, in the Oval Office."

Here again, I didn't see any kind of absurdity or incongruity in this situation. It struck me as the most natural thing in the world, that I should have written a letter to President Nixon and that he should have responded in just this way, and I was so green and innocent it never occurred to me anyone else would see it any different. After all, it's not like he was offering me a job in his administration, or anything so far-fetched as that; it was just a meeting.

The line went silent for a couple beats, and then I heard my mother shouting to my father. "Honey," she called out, "pick up the phone. Something's wrong with Johnny."

It's funny—don't you think?—that such a simple thing as winning an audience with an elected official should be regarded with distrust and disbelief. *Something's wrong with Johnny.* We hear stories like this and reject them as incredible when they should be the order of the day. After all, why shouldn't a president, or a congressman, or a university president make time in his or her busy schedule to meet every thoughtful voter or constituent or student who makes the time to seek him or her out on this or that issue? And yet it was difficult for my mother to conceive that an event of this magnitude had happened to her son. Yes, my parents had raised me to believe that anything was possible, but at the same time this was shocking. An audience with the President of the United States? Who could believe such a thing? But believe it we did, in time.

The call from the White House finally came in on my dormitory phone. I was in the shower at the time, and the person who answered mistook the woman on the phone for my mother. "Hey

Kasich!" he hollered into the bathroom. "It's your old lady on the line!"

I bundled out of the bathroom double-quick, a towel wrapped around my waist, not wanting to keep my mother waiting, only to find President Nixon's personal secretary, Rosemary Woods, on the other end.

I was on a plane to Washington soon after, so full of hope and ideas the plane might have listed to my side of the aisle. I was excited, but calm. Perhaps it was the mailman's son in me, but I had a sheet with directions on it, and a letter of introduction from someone on the President's staff, and I held on to these pieces of paper the entire way there. By the time I got to the visitor's gate outside the White House they were so worn and crumpled from my tight-fisted clutching that they looked like something that had been retrieved from the trash, but I presented them to the guard like they were golden tickets. I announced myself: "I'm here for a meeting with the President."

I've since learned that our meeting—in December 1970—took place the same week as President Nixon's now famous photo opportunity with Elvis Presley, and when I made the connection I thought, How strange! To have been granted an audience with the President just a couple appointments away from his meeting with an American icon?

They let me in soon enough. I was ushered to a reception area outside the Oval Office by some guy in a suit, after which some other guy in a suit came over and filled me in on the drill. He said, "Young man, you're going to get five minutes alone with the President. He'll be ready for you shortly."

I thought, Five minutes? I thought, This guy has got to be kidding! Of course, if I told any lobbyist or journalist or ranking politician that he or she was on the President's calendar for five minutes of face-time, they'd be thrilled. But I wasn't thrilled. No, sir. Far from it. I'd come all this way. My parents had spent all this money—money we didn't really have to spare on such as this. I'd told all my friends. They were going to have to yank me out of this place, because I wasn't leaving after five minutes.

I was led into the Oval Office, and walked across that beautiful blue carpet with the seal of the United States of America, and it felt like I was walking across history. I thought of all the great world leaders who had trod on those very fibers, all the great decisions that had been made in this very room.

The man in the suit made the introductions, stating the obvious: "Mr. President, John Kasich. John Kasich, the President of the United States."

I shook Richard Nixon's hand and sat down across from him. Right at his desk. The same desk I had seen on the news. It was all so powerful, and immediate, and *right there*, and I had never before been inside such an important moment.

And just what did I do, inside that important moment? I talked. I got a few things off my chest. And the President listened. He asked a couple questions, and I offered what I hoped weren't perfunctory answers, and I figured if I just kept talking those five minutes would never quite come on the clock, and as I spoke I allowed myself to think I was making some kind of difference, bending the ear of the leader of the free world on issues that were of profound importance—to me, anyway. It became clear as I talked that he was taking the opportunity to gauge the mood on college campuses, just seven months removed from the shootings at Kent State, but I didn't dwell on his agenda. What mattered to me was the opportunity.

The good news is that meeting lasted about twenty minutes, which I counted as all the time in the world. Think of it: An eighteen-year-old college freshman, alone in the Oval Office with the most powerful man in the world for twenty minutes. Pretty incredible, don't you think? The bad news is I would go on to spend eighteen years in Congress, and if you go back and add up all the time I spent alone in the Oval Office with various presidents you'll see it doesn't come close to those twenty minutes. I guess I peaked out at the age of eighteen. That's when I should have retired.

LOOKING AHEAD

That trip to the White House, and a growing friendship with Novice Fawcett, set the tone for the balance of my four years at Ohio State—and, in many ways, for my future. I majored in political science, with an eye toward a career in law and government. That had always been the plan—although for a time in there, I'll confess, it had been a fallback option. See, in addition to the priesthood, my other childhood goal was to be President of the United States, and as soon as I realized I liked girls too much to seriously consider a life of celibacy I looked to the White House. To be honest, I don't remember giving public voice to such lofty dreams, but after a long political career I keep running into some of my old Buckeye friends who insist I used to introduce myself back at school by telling people I was going to be president someday. I don't remember as much, and I don't like how I come across in these retellings, but I have to consider the evidence. After all, I've heard this from several people over the years, so there must be something to it. I can only hope my fellow students didn't dismiss me back then as some sort of pompous idiot, because my ambition was genuine. It might have been a bit premature, and perhaps even a couple inches out of reach, but it was certainly genuine, and so I set about it, using that White House meeting as an all-important springboard to a series of wonderful summer jobs and internships in Washington leading up to my graduation.

If I have any regrets about my academic career, it's that I never went to law school, because I think it would have helped me enormously in government, but I followed my heart rather than my head and succumbed to the lure of politics. Upon graduation, I stumbled upon a job as an intern in the Ohio legislature, where I would work for several years, soon enough as a Republican aide. In short order, I became convinced that I could be a member of the legislature, and got it in my head to challenge an incumbent in my district named Robert O'Shaughnessy. I was twenty-four years old, and after only a year or two as a legislative aide I'd convinced myself that I could do a better job than any of the folks in elected office. Understand, this was pie-in-the-sky stuff, and Republican officials were fairly stunned by my decision to run against such a formidable opponent. I had no money, no campaign team, no name recognition, no support, and no office. And, once I stepped down from my post as an aide in the legislature to focus on my campaign, I had no real paying job.

To make matters even more intimidating, the O'Shaughnessy name was legendary in and around Columbus. There was a dam named after my opponent's family. A local funeral home also bore his name. He had a brother who had served in the state senate. It was a regular dynasty. Robert O'Shaughnessy himself was the chairman of the Ways and Means Committee, and very much out in front in terms of support and name recognition and things of that nature. In fact, the guy was such a force that no credible Republican candidates seemed to want to step forward to challenge him, so the field was wide open. No one was that big a fool—except of course for me. I gave myself a two-year running start and had at it. I needed every hour of those two years to get my message across. I didn't have the first idea how to go about running a campaign, but I didn't let these things stop me. I just grabbed a phone book and started making some calls, unleashing a tremendous grassroots effort and dragging Robert O'Shaughnessy into the fight of his political life—eventually attracting good people like Don Thibaut to my campaign, because they were impressed with my hard work and willingness to take on any battle.

Now, I should mention here that I got married soon after graduation—to my first wife, Mary Lee, who was tremendously supportive of my decision to seek office. But I was so consumed by the campaign and my new job as a candidate that we were soon like two ships passing in the night, a prescription for disaster in any marriage. What it came down to, really, was time: I'd set things up so that I didn't have any. Plain and simple, I neglected my marriage. I did not tend to the garden, or work diligently at whatever nurturing metaphor you care to slot in here, because I was too busy trying to get a toehold in the legislature. Fortunately, there were no children involved, and we could both read the handwriting on the wall clearly enough to recognize we were headed down the wrong road, so we parted friends and went our separate ways.

And so, let me be perfectly clear: If you're looking for the pure individual who practices what he preaches, who never makes mistakes, who has no recognizable failings or shortcomings or deep, dark secrets . . . you won't find him here. I'm human, same as everyone else. Sometimes I get it right, and sometimes I don't, and most times I'm able to catch myself in time to set things right. Hopefully, I learn from my missteps and don't repeat them.

In any case, my poor mother was devastated when I filed for divorce; she was so morally and philosophically opposed to it that I think she would have had an easier time of it if I'd told her I'd robbed a bank, but I hadn't robbed a bank so she had to find it in her heart to forgive me. And she did, just as I have found it in my heart to forgive myself—for being young, and rash, and totally unprepared for the full-time commitment of marriage and family.

Enough said.

I was swallowed up by the campaign, and because I gave myself a two-year head start, for a time in there I didn't know if I could make ends meet. I can still remember being pulled over for speeding in the small town of Worthington, Ohio, and as the police officer came to the car I emptied my pockets in a gesture intended to pull some sympathy and maybe get off with just a warning. I told the police officer who I was, and that I was running for state senate. I presented him with my driver's license, and a quarter, which was all the money I could find in my wallet or my pockets. I said, "Officer, if you give me a fine you may put an end to my campaign because this is all I've got."

(No doubt I carried the quarter on my mother's good counsel, on the sound thinking that if my car broke down I'd at least be able to call someone for help. And I must have caught the cop on a good day, because he let me off with just a warning.)

It really was a shoestring operation—a lot like starting a small business and putting everything you have into it and hoping for the best, only here my hope for the best wasn't for myself alone. I truly felt that the time had come for a change, and that I was the man for the job. Had there been another, more experienced, better-backed Republican candidate, I might have determined that he or she was more suited to it, but there was no one else. The fighter in me could not let this guy go unchallenged.

A word or two on that fighter in me: I had been a small, scrappy kid. Even as an adult, I check in on the short side of most weight charts. I was taught to work twice as hard as the next guy, often to get half as far, and I am reminded here of those long summer afternoons playing baseball up at the schoolyard. We've all experienced those afternoons, right? Running around in the hot sun, lapping at the water from the nearest garden hose like it was a little piece of heaven. I was one of the smaller kids, so I got in the habit of running my mouth off a bit in order to be taken seriously. That's where I think I got my argumentative streak, on the ball field. I never gave up on an argument. When I thought the ball was out, and everyone else thought the ball was fair, and it was the bottom of the last inning and we were about to lose the game, and we had been playing the game for hours and hours . . . well, I just wouldn't give in, the same way I wouldn't give in on this race for the state senate.

PERSISTENCE PAYS

Sure enough, there were a handful of other Republican candidates who emerged as the election grew near, but there was no one with any real experience or any real shot at winning—not that I had any either. So I kept at it. For nearly two straight years, seven days a week, sometimes around the clock, I kept pecking away at Robert O'Shaughnessy. I took time off to sleep, and that was it. I drove a red Chevette at the time, and I practically lived in it. The back seat was littered with campaign literature and fast food wrappers and a change of clothes, although most of the time the change of clothes had already been put to use, which meant there was usually just a small pile of laundry. If I wasn't in somebody's home pitching my candidacy, I was at a rally or a press conference or a community event of some kind. Or I was going door-to-door, or cold-calling on the phone, or trapping fliers beneath the windshield wipers of parked cars at the local mall. The 15th was a fairly big district back in those days, with over 300,000 people, which meant I had to knock on a whole lot of doors, but that's just what I did.

The cold calls were interesting. Few people were doing that kind of thing—and certainly no one in Ohio. I wrote my own script, and tried to stick to it. I didn't have volunteers making the calls or visits on my behalf, at least not in the beginning. I just pulled a number from the phone book, or knocked on the door of the next house down the street, and introduced myself. "Hi," I'd say. "My name's John Kasich, and I'm running for state senate in two years." Then I set about earnestly and aggressively pitching my message.

And somehow, in the doing, folks sparked to my campaign. Money started to come in. Volunteers started to sign on. At some point, Republican Party leaders began to smell that I could actually win this thing, so they started throwing some money and support my way as well, and when Robert O'Shaughnessy finally looked up and began to take me seriously I was at mile 25 of our 26.2 mile marathon, and he was gasping for air back at mile 23.

He had no idea how many miles I'd run, how much work I'd put in, how much support I'd gained along the way. If he'd thought about me at all, it was very likely as a joke. I was just a kid. When he finally saw me as a real threat, there was no time to catch up.

Election night was pure pandemonium. The weekend before the election, the local newspapers had some flattering things to say about my campaign and about my potential, but none of the pundits figured I could pull it off. In fact, they all thought I would lose by a significant margin. The O'Shaughnessy name was too tough to beat, they all said. As it played out, though, the election wasn't even close. I ended up with better than 56 percent of the vote, a giant margin in a contest like this—and a stunning victory. Took the entire state by surprise to where some folks started calling it the biggest upset in the history of the Ohio legislature. Took poor O'Shaughnessy by surprise, too, and caught him napping. To many people, it was as stunning as when Buster Douglas (another Columbus underdog) knocked out Mike Tyson for the heavyweight title. It was wonderful. My parents couldn't have been more proud. To them, it was another rung on that ever-reaching ladder of success. I had climbed higher than any Kasich before me, higher than my coal miner grandfather could have ever imagined.

Granted, all I'd gotten for all that climbing was a thankless elected position that paid a mere $17,500—but to me, just then, that was all the money I needed. Heck, it was all the money in the world, but it wasn't about the money. The good guys don't go into politics to get rich or famous. They do it to make a difference, and I counted myself as one of the good guys. I was out to make a difference. To matter. To stand for something.

And I was determined to keep my promises, which meant

making some noise right away. Don Thibaut became my top aide and he remains a close confidant, and together we hit the ground running. I learned how to work with other people. I learned how to get things done in a two-party system. I learned how to compromise when appropriate, and how to form alliances. I learned how to communicate with my constituents. And I learned how to write a budget. When my own party decided to raise taxes, I wrote my own budget that addressed the fiscal problems of the state and allowed me to avoid breaking one of my chief campaign promises—namely, an unwillingness to raise taxes. It angered my new colleagues, and I got slaughtered with it, but that didn't bother me. In fact, I was just pleased that I had a chance to present it. (Indeed, many of my provisions were eventually enacted, which I took as a silver-lining-type compliment.) It was the only budget I ever wrote in the legislature, but it would begin a pattern of going out on my own limb and crunching my own numbers that I would continue in the U.S. House of Representatives.

Very quickly, I earned a reputation as someone who didn't play by any fixed set of rules. My new colleagues didn't quite know what to make of me. First time I stood up in the caucus and made an impassioned speech about some issue or other one of the state senators took me aside afterward and said, "Put a little mustard on that hot dog, Senator"—meaning, I guess, that I had a flair for the melodramatic. The message from my own party, early on, was that I was "irresponsible," which is the word that gets tossed around when you refuse to go along with the establishment. I was irresponsible because I broke from the party to present my own budget. I was irresponsible because I voted my conscience over the party line. I was irresponsible because I eschewed favoritism and cronyism and isms of every stripe. I was irresponsible because

I turned back a proposed pay raise that was presented during one of my first sessions, because that had been one of my campaign promises.

There I was, meaning to keep my word, and the legislature went and voted itself a pay raise, so I refused the money. It was a $5,000 raise, so it was more than just a token gesture; it was significant money, especially when set against my $17,500 starting salary, and I had to jump through all kinds of hoops just to refuse it. I even had to pay taxes on it—and, of course, to shoulder the disdain of my fellow senators who didn't quite know what to make of this brash young kid who seemed determined to make them look bad in the eyes of their constituents by turning back what may or may not have been a deserved pay raise. I did this more than once, actually—and you have to realize, it wasn't a one-time bump in pay. It was $5,000 every year, so it ran to a lot of money. I started to worry that people might think me stupid for turning back all that money; heck, *I* started to think I might be stupid for turning back all that money, but I stuck to my principles. Even when I got to Congress, and my new colleagues voted themselves a raise of their own, I refused it. I wouldn't be one of those "vote no and take the dough" officials. I meant to keep my word—only after eight years of giving back all this money, and paying all these excess taxes, it seemed a little besides the point. I kept voting against the raises, but I finally stopped refusing them, because I realized I was beating my head against the wall. Nobody seemed to care except me, so I moved on to something else.

All of which takes me in a not-so-roundabout way to the front porch of my career in government, which eventually included nine terms as a U.S. congressman and an uplifting but ultimately unsuccessful run for the 2000 Republic Party presidential nomination that eventually went to George W. Bush. It was uplifting to me, anyway, and I took great satisfaction from the fact that no one dismissed me out of hand. No one laughed. Little Johnny Kasich, from McKees Rocks, Pennsylvania, throwing his hat into the biggest ring in the free world, and it was all within reach: a lifelong dream, close enough to taste. I might never have been anything more than a long shot, and I might have run through my meager campaign fund before the first primary, but I attracted some good people to the effort. In fact, Ed Gillespie, who went on to become the chairman of the Republican National Committee, was my press secretary. Ed Goeas was my pollster, and he's one of the best in the business. Don Fierce, the noted Republican strategist who actually talked me into running in the first place, and Karen Johnson, a high-ranking political veteran, also signed on to the effort—which I took as a great barometer.

ON MY WAY

I set out these backstories for the way they signal what I'm about, what motivates me, what it's taken for me to get things done and make a difference. Too, I set them out for the way they show how things were, up against how things have become. And I set them out for the way they remind me never to get too full of myself, or to take too terribly much for granted or forget where I've come from, because bundled up and taken together these are the things that define me. This is who I've strived to be—and how I've gone about some of that striving.

That said, this book is not intended as political memoir. It is not an autobiography. It is, however, deeply personal. It's a think piece on what's ailing America, and yet it's not one of those conservative manifestos we've lately seen filling our bookstore shelves, even though if I had to categorize some of my views along the spectrum of social commentary I'd allow that I'm more right than left, more traditional than contemporary, more red than blue. I don't mean to start a partisan dialogue in these pages so much as to generate a free-flowing discussion on the state of our union, and to do so effectively I believe I need to bring myself to the table. That's where it gets personal. The societal drift I wrote of earlier doesn't recognize party lines; the values that have done their level best to define me are not the exclusive domain of a former Republican congressman from one of our flyover states; and the outrage I'll voice at the greed, corruption, cynicism, sloth, and duplicity plaguing our American institutions is not mine alone, even if it comes from that deeply personal place.

Honesty, integrity, personal responsibility, faith, humility, accountability, compassion, forgiveness . . . these are our American values, our common denominators, and in the pages ahead I'll offer my take on how to reclaim them and set them loose once again in the areas of politics, business, education, religion, sports, and popular culture.

Here goes . . .

3

TAKING A STAND ON GOVERNMENT

"Politics is not an end, but a means. It is not a product, but a process. It is the art of government. Like other values it has its counterfeits. So much emphasis has been placed upon the false that the significance of the true has been obscured and politics has come to convey the meaning of crafty and cunning selfishness, instead of candid and sincere service."

Calvin Coolidge

I'll open this one with a caution and a story. First, the caution: This is *not* intended to be a political book. It's a book about how we live and work and think, and how we might do a better job of all three in order to make our country a better place. And it's no autobiography, either, although I recognize that in order to make a compelling point I must sometimes offer an insight or example from my personal experience. For good or ill, I have lived a political life; most of my personal experience has been in and around government, so it's only natural that a great many of my insights and examples will be pulled from this arena. It's a little like stating the obvious, I know, but I mention it here at the outset because I don't want readers to feel they've been duped into buying a partisan diatribe from some washed-up pol.

Now, the story: I was having dinner with a group of people the weekend before the 2004 presidential election, which as you'll recall was a polarizing time in this country. Everything was reduced to black and white—or, I should say, to red and blue. John Kerry was the devil incarnate to Republicans, and George Bush was the devil incarnate to Democrats, and there was no room in the debate to consider each man on his own merits, nor each issue on its face. It was as if the fate of the world hung in the balance. Leaders of each party whipped Americans into such a hyperventilated frenzy that otherwise intelligent Republicans started to believe that if Kerry won the White House America would cease to exist, while Democrats felt sure that if Bush retained the White House we were all doomed.

And so it was in the eye of the storm of this blind partisanship that this dinner took place, and at one point during an otherwise pleasant evening a well-dressed, well-spoken, and presumably well-informed woman asked me what would happen if John Kerry won. The very thought was anathema to this concerned woman, that's how stirred up she was over the election, so I looked at her and calmly said, "The country will be fine."

"What do you mean?" she shot back, aghast. She knew I was a Republican, and she knew I cared deeply about the future of this country, and I guess she thought I'd share her concern over the grim prospect of a Kerry administration. She couldn't get that I was so calm over something as dire as this election—which, as we were endlessly reminded, was the mother of all elections.

"Well," I said, "the Republicans would still control the House and the Senate. The bench would slowly become more liberal. And there'd probably be less spending, because the Republicans would reject most of Kerry's programs."

The woman looked at me like I had just given her permission to breathe a long sigh. "You mean it won't be the end of America as we know it?" she said.

"No, ma'am," I assured her. "America will survive."

Then she thanked me profusely for setting her mind at ease, and told me how much better she felt, how much more hopeful, and I realized she might have been over the top but she wasn't alone. There were a great many Americans out there who were moving to Canada over the outcome of that election, either way, because the campaign took on such a heated and heightened tone. It was more than just ugly—it was downright incendiary. Even the *New York Times* reported on Democrats suffering from post-election stress syndrome following Bush's victory, complete with note and comment from area mental health professionals on how to cope over the next four years. I read that and thought (with at least a couple shades of sarcasm), Well, if the paper of record is weighing in on it, then it must be a certifiable phenomenon.

No question, we were well manipulated into believing the 2004 presidential election was the most important election of our lifetime, which it may well have been, but we can be certain that when the 2008 election rolls around it will also be the most important election of our lifetime. And here's a news flash: In 2012, it'll be the same story all over again.

Now, here's another news flash for you—and this one troubles me even more than the last one: We haven't seen middle ground for so long I'm no longer certain it still exists. I can't help but think that the deepening divide between conservatives and liberals in this country can be traced to an alarming lack of backbone among our elected leaders. Yes, there are exceptions to every sweeping, alarmist statement I might make in these pages, but for the most part politicians today are more concerned with being *politically* correct than they are with being merely correct, and more likely to take a back seat than any kind of stand. More and more, our elected officials are accomplishing less and less— all because they have become so deathly afraid of offending any group or individual that they wind up doing nothing much at all but more of the same.

WHY POLITICS MATTERS

Before I go any further on this, I want to state for the record that our democratic form of government is the best thing going. Our Founding Fathers got it right, and within the framework of our democracy there is room for leadership and courage and vision and all those good things that make this country great and strong. Heck, we depend on leaders with courage and vision to keep us headed down the right road, but from time to time there's a vacuum. From time to time, we find ourselves in a state of such profound drift we get to wondering if we'll ever see our way to the other side, and these days we appear to be drifting. We've gotten to where it's too difficult for our elected officials to go it alone, to make tough decisions, to reach across the aisle and develop friendships and alliances with members of the opposing party. It's too difficult to fight the status quo. In fact, that's become one of the most effective ways to move up in the leadership of your party—to become a party guy. Power for power's sake. Obsession with reelection. The rising influence of special interests that keep otherwise honest politicians from taking an honest, objective view on a variety of issues. That's the worst of politics, and it puts me in mind of the opening line of Charles Dickens's *A Tale of Two Cities*—"It was the best of times, it was the worst of times"—and leaves me thinking we have to fumble through these bad patches until we find some firmer footing.

The political pendulum swings back and forth in this country, and right now we're at the troubling end of its arc. I've spent most of my adult life in politics and I've pretty much seen it all. The good, the bad, the downright ugly. What astounds me these days is how far we've veered off a principled course, how we've let things slip to where politics is no longer about doing good but about winning elections and destroying your opponent. Local politics, state politics, national politics . . . it's all the same. The stakes might change as you move up the ladder; the headlines might get a little bigger and the falls from grace a little steeper, but at bottom our current political system is all about what stripes you wear and whose side you're on and where your bread is buttered. Forgive, please, the tired metaphors but I can think of no better way to describe such a tired arrangement. Lately, I find myself cringing at the venom and vitriol that passes for spirited debate, and at the way our elected leaders seem unable to tolerate their fundamental differences. It's gotten ugly.

Of course, political intrigue and smear tactics are nothing new, and you can find distressing parallels between our modern elections and some of the (quite literal) backstabbing and infighting that went on in ancient Roman times, but things seem to have kicked up a notch with the advent of C-SPAN coverage and twenty-four-hour cable news channels, to where the venom and vitriol have gotten away from us.

Nowadays, backroom negotiations and eleventh-hour deal making are considered fodder for the political pundits and the news junkies, and even the smallest initiative is subject to the kind of big-time second-guessing that can swing an election or kill a sound proposal. Good candidates are discouraged from even seeking office because they haven't lived campaign-perfect lives (translation: they smoked marijuana in college, opposed the war in Vietnam, failed to declare wages paid to a domestic employee, or committed some other unforgivable transgression or crime against polite society), while weak candidates are propped up by party leaders as the best and the brightest when in truth they might just be the least objectionable. It's enough to make you question how we even manage to *function* as a society, let alone thrive.

Unfortunately, I don't see anyone out there on our political landscape likely to stand against the tide of all these negatives. Not just yet, anyway. The prevailing strategy seems to be to ride it all out and hope for the best, but that's not any kind of strategy. That's wishful thinking, and wishful thinking is simply not going to get us anywhere close to where we need to be on this— not anytime soon. We need true and effective and inspiring leadership. We need for our elected officials to stand once again for America. And we need these things now more than ever before. We need our politicians to rail against the status quo, and to put the best interests of our children and grandchildren ahead of their own interests. We need to turn sharply from a system that grants our candidates and their party backers the right to cut each other's legs out from under them, to pander for votes and peddle their influence, and to slick-package the truth and the public interest in such a way that it bolsters their campaigns. Like it or not—and here I check in on the side of *not*, in case you were wondering—politics has become a blood sport; it's all about winning, and only a little bit about governing, and to my thinking the balance is all off.

STANDING TALL

Integrity isn't a virtue you hear all that much about in our various branches of government, and not because it's a given (which, of course, it *should* be) but because it's so uncommon. I served in Congress with a principled man named Tim Penny. He was a Democrat from Minnesota whose frustration with Washington politics reached a tipping point when President Clinton proposed a big tax increase with few spending cuts, going against his own campaign promise. Tim had enough with empty Washington rhetoric, so what did he do? He quit, that's what he did. You might think, Well, what in the world did that accomplish? In the short term, probably not a whole lot. The folks in Tim's congressional district lost a good man in Washington, so on the surface Tim Penny's response to Bill Clinton's about-face actually cost the good people back home, but very quickly Tim took on a kind of folk-hero status—in Congress, in Minnesota, and across this great land. His stature grew enormously, simply because he took a stand. He was disillusioned with Clinton's plan, and with a political system that seemed bound to support it; more to the point, he didn't like how Clinton promised one thing and then went out and did another, so he stood against it.

Tim Penny went on to run for governor, and he was defeated, but that could never diminish his reputation for doing the right thing. We'll hear from him again, believe me, because this country needs good people who sound off against injustice and cowardice and avarice, folks like Tim who call it like they see it—and then go out and do something about it.

Like Tim, I find this sea change in such groupthink-type political perspective more than a little offensive—and what most offends me as an American citizen is the way we've allowed that us-versus-them mentality to take hold. I repeat myself, I know, but it's an all-important point. It's the defining rift of our times, and on some very basic level at least it all comes back to those C-SPAN cameras, and that round-the-clock news coverage, and that win-at-all-costs approach in our campaigns. Or maybe it's the blind reliance on pollsters and focus groups. Whatever it is, we've gotten to where the middle ground has collapsed around us, and we've been left on either edge of the precipice—afraid to take a step in *any* direction.

To some people, *compromise* has become a dirty word in politics, but I don't see it quite that way. Tim Penny didn't see it that way, either. To compromise doesn't mean to sell out. It doesn't mean that you sacrifice your principles. It doesn't mean that you bend to every special interest other than your constituents'. It means listening to the opinions of others, and respecting those opinions, and recognizing the value in searching for solutions built on consensus—and yet it's within this great divide that we find many of the root ills of our political system.

In my own career, very early on, I was constantly pressured by party leaders or legislative and congressional colleagues to toe this or that line, and I did my level best to ignore such coercion and lead with my gut. I would not be told how to vote or what to say, and yet there was significant pressure to do just that—on just about a daily basis. A couple weeks after I was elected to the Ohio state senate, for just one example, I was called to the governor's office for a meeting on real estate taxes. The governor was a Republican, and a man I came to admire, but we differed on this one. He was proposing that there be no more voting on real estate taxes, and I thought this was just outrageous. I couldn't even begin to understand the governor's position. I mean, how can you put real estate taxes on the table without giving the people a chance to weigh in on it?

So there I was, all of twenty-six years old, sitting around the governor's desk with a bunch of men all fifteen or twenty years older than me (at least!), and I wasn't about to be intimidated. We were all eating take-out hamburgers from Wendy's, as we always did in these meetings because the governor was a shareholder, and I sat there with that wax fast food paper in my lap, waiting for one of the more senior legislators to say something, but when no one did I spoke up. I said, "Governor, I can't vote for something like that. It's just not right."

Let me tell you, I would have gotten a warmer response if I'd suggested that McDonald's hamburgers were tastier than Wendy's. The office fell silent, and the governor shot me this icy stare to put me in my place. My position may have been right and just, but it certainly wasn't appreciated. Realize, I had already (and quite publicly) refused a pay raise, and now I was standing against this proposal on real estate taxes, and these people had probably heard just about enough out of this junior legislator.

I found myself in another tense meeting just a few weeks later, with a group of local judges who were pushing for a pay raise of their own—this at a time when state employees were feeling the economic strain of a decades-old wage scale. I'd thought I was attending a dinner to discuss various issues affecting the community, but as the evening wore on it was clear this pay raise was all the judges wanted to talk about. I finally said, "Gentlemen, I'm not going to vote for a pay raise for judges until our state employees get a raise."

If any one of these guys had a gavel, he would have had at it and cited me with contempt of court. As it happened, all I got was their contempt. The judges started screaming at me, and telling me I would never amount to anything in politics, and kicking up the kind of dust you don't normally see at such distinguished heels. One judge, with tongue only partly in cheek, suggested that if I ever got into any kind of trouble, I'd better be sure it wasn't in his Franklin County jurisdiction. Man, these people were just furious with me, and I'm not sure I was right and that the judges weren't entitled to pay raises for all their hard work and good counsel, but I told them what I thought. It was a priority to these judges, but only on a personal level; in my mind the lower-level state employees had to come first.

MR. KASICH GOES TO WASHINGTON (AGAIN)

At the end of my four-year term as a state senator, I was faced with a difficult decision—owing mainly to redistricting. I could challenge one of the few mentors I'd cultivated in the legislature, a veteran state senator named Ted Gray who had gone out of his way to ease some of my growing pains as a young legislator. Or, I could run for Congress. I couldn't see running a campaign against a friend and mentor who had helped me put my experiences in valuable perspective, so I made the decision to move on, running my congressional campaign as a sitting state senator, and as I did I looked back on some of the lessons I'd learned in the legislature. I realized I'd developed enormous respect for people who were fighters. It didn't matter to me if they were Republicans or Democrats. It didn't matter if we stood on the same side of a given issue. What mattered was whether or not they were principled, whether they fought for their values and beliefs. We might have differed on certain issues, but there was a mutual respect. I wouldn't go so far as to call these relationships *friendships*, mind you, because of the old saw that suggests if you want a friend in politics you should buy a dog, but I had a good working relationship with several of our most liberal legislators, and it is only underneath such mutual respect that you can begin to explore common ground, and I set off for Washington in search of that common ground—not really having any idea what I would find.

When I first told my dad I was going to run for office, he suggested I consider a career in banking instead. I don't think he fully appreciated my impulse, but as I stated earlier, I went into politics to change the world. My family and friends in McKees Rocks had never known anyone in politics—and the idea that someone could be driven to make big, positive changes was unfamiliar to them because they didn't know it firsthand. But they knew me, and they knew my mother's determination to "fight City Hall" must have rubbed off on me, so I had their full support. They knew that my heart was in, around, and all over the right place, and that I meant to make a difference. I wasn't out to play games or go through the motions of party loyalty, and if I saw a clear path toward a solution to a given problem that happened to meander through territory of my more liberal colleagues I meant to take it.

We're all driven by our own impulses, and there are as many different justifications to seeking office as there are candidates doing the seeking, and yet I maintain that a great majority of the people who initially set out for a career in politics do so for reasons that are noble and admirable. It's what happens next that's got me so concerned. You know, I have a good friend who was recently elected to the United States Senate. He spent millions to get elected, and he ran a good, straightforward campaign. I called to congratulate him not long after he took office, and before we had a chance to talk about our families or our golf games or anything else, he wanted to know how he could start raising more money for his reelection campaign. That's the great catch-22 of our political system, isn't it? You need money to win elections— and yet it's the reliance on money that gets us into trouble, and it's the insatiable desire for more and more of it that ultimately limits independence. For the most part, you get your money from the people who have it, and by and large too much of that money comes from special interest groups. The key here, though, is that just because someone or some group gives money to your campaign, it doesn't mean they own you. Like every other politician in Washington, I took money from special interest groups, but in my case it never amounted to much, and as time went on these special interest groups were less and less inclined to contribute to my campaigns because they could never count on getting anything in return. I worked hard to ensure that the money never got in the way of my good judgment, but a lot of folks don't make that effort, and when you have these huge gobs of money it begins to whittle down the system. It takes the edge off someone's ability to make an honest assessment of a situation.

Today, a mounting federal deficit and growing holes in our Social Security, Medicare, and other entitlement programs are threatening a financial meltdown, and the Bush administration is up against it. These are the front-burner issues of our day, but early on in my tenure in Washington we were facing a whole other muddle. I landed on the Defense Committee during my first few terms in Congress, which back then meant planning and plotting against the Russians. Six years into my tenure, I joined the Budget Committee, because I knew from my days in the Ohio legislature that the budget drives everything. I remember going to my first Budget Committee meeting like it was yesterday. I was stunned. On the Defense Committee, everybody sort of got along; for the most part, we all wanted to beat the Communists and there wasn't much partisanship. On the Budget Committee, though, folks were tearing each other's arms off. Every line item, or just about, was a fierce battle.

I'll get back to my work on the Defense Committee in just a bit, but I want to spend some time on the budget process because I think it's instructive. I was overwhelmed at how little there was to fight over, because both budgets were deeply flawed proposals. Bush the First, his budget was terrible. And the Democratic budget was even worse. So I went back to my office and announced to my staff that we would write our own budget. They looked at me like I had blown a gasket, but I was dead serious. Why? Well, I happened to believe in balanced budgets, plain and simple. The business of government should be a value business just like any other. How can you go year after year, spending more than you take in? You just can't. What about our responsibility to our children? We can't saddle all these succeeding generations with an insurmountable debt just because it's easier than achieving present-day accountability, and yet for too long that had been the default course.

THE BOTTOM LINES

The White House had the vast resources of the federal government working on its budget. The Democrats had hundreds of people crunching numbers on their version. In my office, we had six people on the job, and before we rolled up our sleeves and got down to it I said in all seriousness, "Well, we might be slightly overstaffed, but I think we can work it out."

And we did. We worked our tails off to get it done, but we got it done and managed to present a real budget with real changes, and if you check the *Congressional Record* you'll see that in 1989 there was offered on the House floor the President's budget, and the Democrats' rebuttal budget, and the Kasich budget. Understand, a budget needs 218 votes out of a possible 435 to win passage, and the party in power always tends to prevail in these things. In actual practice, the budgeting process is a whole lot like a WWE Smackdown; it gets interesting and heated at times, but you always know how it's going to turn out. It's a very partisan endeavor. In these days of wall-to-wall television coverage, they flash the votes up on the screen for God and country to consider, so everyone knows where their elected officials stand, but back in 1989 that was not yet the case. (Actually, C-SPAN had been doing its thing since 1979, but folks weren't watching in any kind of big way, and we'd yet to see all those cable news channels devoted to analyzing every nuance from the House floor, the way we see today.) We voted first on the Democratic budget. They were in the majority at that time, and they received 230 votes. Then we voted on the Bush budget, which received 213 votes, falling just short. The Kasich budget received 30 votes of approval.

I went back to my office to talk to my staff after the vote. Everyone was deeply depressed. I said, "What's wrong with you people? Are you crazy? I'm a mailman's son, and we just had twenty-nine other elected members of Congress vote to adopt our budget to run the United States government. That's fantastic, and we're just getting started."

Every year I offered my own budget for consideration, and by the third or fourth year my budget received more votes than the President got for his budget, and in so doing I learned a few things about leadership. Leadership is not talking. Leadership is doing. Every time they beat my budget on the floor of the House and I lay there in a bloody heap, people knew I was committed. It wasn't talk. It was action. The other great thing about leadership is this: You can't accomplish anything without a team. And, if you have a righteous cause people will come to that cause. I don't care what it is. Little by little, year by year, my team built bigger and stronger and more viable budgets—each of them fiscally, socially, morally, and even politically responsible—and as a result of these efforts I leaped over seven other congressmen more senior than me to become the senior Republican on the Budget Committee. And then in 1995 when the Republicans won the majority I became chairman of the House Budget Committee and I thought, Okay, we're cooking now. We were poised and ready to balance the budget for the first time since man walked on the moon—and I was right there in the middle of it, mixing it up, making a difference.

As it happened, President Clinton wanted to phony up the numbers on this first go-round, so we shut down the government. Today, with perspective, pundits look back and suggest that shutting down the government under those circumstances was dumb, but I look back and think it was one of the greatest moments of my career. Why? Well, typically, politicians make their decisions based on votes. They'll side this way or that way on an issue according to public opinion polls and reelection concerns. And yet in at least this one instance politicians set aside these concerns and stood up for what was right. For our children. For our shared future. For America. For this one battle, for the time being, we forgot about politics and focused on good government, and if we had to take a beating for it then so be it. And as a direct result of that government shutdown in 1995, we wrote a bill that provided for the first balanced budget in nearly forty years and allowed us to pay down the largest chunk of our staggering national debt in the history of this country. In all, not too bad for a guy who started out with only thirty votes in support of his first budget.

Regrettably, we've increased the national debt at an unbelievably alarming rate, and along the way we've blown the opportunity to take some of our surpluses and put them to work saving some of our biggest, most essential social programs. But we were on it, for a while. We had it covered, for a while, until we let ourselves be swayed by a new agenda that had almost nothing to do with fiscal responsibility.

Looking back, I'm as proud of my work on the Budget Committee as I am of anything else I did in government—and that pride runs well beyond the bottom line on the balanced budget we eventually put forward. It's about something more than just patting ourselves on the back, and here it is: For a brief, shining moment, our system was firing on all cylinders, and working the way it was meant to work, and I count myself lucky to have been a part of it. Realize, beginning in 1993, when our committee first came together from all different parts of the country, representing all different interests and all different political perspectives and agendas, we made a concerted effort to look past our conflicting interests and work toward a common goal. We were from New York, and Ohio, and the South, and the Pacific Northwest. There was even a congressman on our committee from Iowa who didn't understand New York City and everything it represented, contending that New Yorkers could never understand the economy of the West—and on this, he was probably right.

COMING TOGETHER, COMING APART

But even though we came from all points on the American compass, we recognized that it was our job to offer some type of direction for our shared economic future, and so we looked at one another and made a decision that we would all hang together or we would simply hang. And it was something to see, the way these dug-in politicians were good to their word. One by one, they gave up programs and expenditures that had been a high priority for them going into this process—in many cases, items that were critical to their reelections—and I watched them stand tall in the name of doing something for our children, for our shared future. For America. Indeed, we watched one another take beating after beating from our local newspapers back home. We shut down the government and took turns being mocked and criticized by our constituents. But we didn't break. We didn't bend. We lowered our heads and got it done, and at the other end we came to understand the power of team, the power of sacrifice, and the power of government when it's able to set aside all these other interests and give folks a chance to demonstrate courage and commitment.

Sad to say, we've drifted from that great, shining moment, and I look on now from my sideline perspective and wonder what will happen next. You can only march an army so far before it has to stop to rest, recharge, and reconnoiter, and right now we're stuck waiting for someone to get us marching again. Right now, the pendulum has swung back toward the wicked part of politics—staying in power, worshipping reelection, caring only about party loyalty, not associating with the other side, always wanting to be right—and it's all made worse by these so-called political pundits who have lately come to inform our national debate on any number of issues.

Just who are these people? They've never held office, never run for office, and yet they loom as armchair quarterbacks, pontificating in black-and-white on complex issues that don't lend themselves to simple solutions. If you're not in there doing it, then you can't really understand what it's all about. These folks start moving the public into silos, painting everyone who dares to disagree with them as the enemy. In radio, they call it narrowcasting, when a talk show is targeted to a specific demographic such as conservative middle-class males, making it easier and more cost-effective for advertisers to reach out to their intended audience. In reality, I call it divisive—and it's a self-fulfilling prophecy. The pundits and analysts and experts start lining up their supporters and putting them into these silos, and the next thing we know we're all of us lined up against one another, unable to see another point of view because we've surrounded ourselves with all these like-minded perspectives. The constant drumbeat of this us-versus-them-type message leaves us all thinking our point of view is the only point of view, and that anyone who takes an opposing view is somehow un-American.

In the middle of all this, we now have a federal deficit that once again threatens to choke our government and our economy, a Social Security system that's melting down, a health care system that's floundering at best, retirees losing their pensions, and on and on. Heck, General Motors may end up declaring bankruptcy if it can't figure out how to deal with its health care costs, that's how far we've fallen, and it's threatening the financial security of this country. My daughters' future! And I'm bitter about it, because it doesn't have to be this way. I was privileged to see firsthand that it doesn't have to be that way, and I mean to shine a light on that privilege so that others might see it as a kind of beacon.

Our Founding Fathers got it right, didn't they? Limited government. The strength and character of our elected officials. This is what politics is all about. At times, it'll fire on all cylinders and consider the public interest ahead of the special interest; it'll weigh the future ahead of the present. Our politicians will get it right. They'll stand up even when people are threatening to burn down their homes, and they'll bring about equal rights. They'll stand up and vote for the cuts and changes in the federal budget, in order to get it balanced. I've seen it happen, and I will see it again. Someone will alight on our political land-scape and give that army some new marching orders. It's just that I don't see it happening anytime soon, which I guess means that things have to get a little worse before they start getting better. Perhaps it's only in moments of profound crisis that our leaders feel empowered to rise up against the tide of conventional think-ing, and maybe we're just not there yet. That's where we're headed, and I worry that the solutions of tomorrow are going to be a whole lot more difficult to achieve than if we had some strong leadership in place today, but that pendulum will swing back before too long and it will be all to the good. That army will be refreshed and resume its march, and folks will once again come together and stand tall and accomplish great things. You can count on it.

THE B-2 BATTLE

Now, let me amend what I wrote earlier about my time on the Defense Committee: It's not entirely accurate to suggest that *everybody* got along because we were united against a common enemy. In addition to the Russians, there was another enemy working against U.S. interests at the time, and that was the sta-tus quo. It's the number one drag on our bottom line—in *every* arena, and in the political arena it can be a real party killer. I may have been strong on defense, but at the same time I was openly critical of the excess spending in every aspect of the federal bud-get, which cast me as a kind of cheap hawk and served to essen-tially alienate me from everyone on both sides of every argument, and made for more than a few tense moments with colleagues who had no room in their thinking for shades of gray.

And, as astonished as I was to discover some of the wasteful spending in the Pentagon budget, I was even more astonished that hardly anyone was speaking out against it. The mantra in Washington at the time was to trim the fat from our social welfare and entitlement programs. But to take the welfare out of the Pentagon? Well, that was tantamount to signing my own pink slip. And to do so as a cheap hawk Republican, who walked the political tightrope of being strong on defense and tight with a dollar, was pretty much like walking the streets of Washington with a "Kick Me!" sign taped to my back. One of my congressional colleagues even called me a traitor to our country, that's how *out there* my position seemed to be among the hawks in the Republican Party, but my feeling was that we needed to ferret out this waste no matter where we found it—and if it cost me some political currency then that would be a small price to pay.

Not incidentally, I thought about jumping across the table and punching the guy who called me a traitor, at a budget meeting in Newt Gingrich's office, but even I could see this would not have been a good career move. To be sure, it was one of the seminal moments of my time in office, and it remains so because I chose to take the high road and rise above all that party line nonsense. I let the comment hang there and sink in, and then I looked at this guy and said, "You'll be lying in bed tonight, and you won't be able to get your own words out of your head. You'll regret what you said, and you'll want to call me and apologize, but let me save you the trouble. I forgive you. I'm not mad. You just don't know any better."

Clearly, it was not considered good politics to go up against the pro-defense lobby, especially for a Republican, but I didn't think it was good government to keep signing off on these ridiculous expenditures. Most ridiculous of all, I came to think, was the development of the B-2 stealth bomber, which at the outset was presented as an essential weapon against the Soviets. I used to listen to the B-2 proponents, spinning all their tales of gloom and doom, and glory and might, and get the feeling I had stepped into some overproduced Cold War action movie. In any given year, the development of the B-2 was a relatively small line item in the overall defense budget, but the long-term plans for the bomber would be realized at a staggering cost, over time. At anywhere from $1 billion to $2 billion per plane, it seemed a colossal misuse of taxpayer monies—and a misguided defense strategy, to boot—and I never understood why we needed to fly a plane around inside the Soviet Union in the middle of a nuclear war, just to drop some more nukes! It made no sense. As I understood it, one nuke was enough to give the Russians a really bad day, so why spend all this money on overkill? And we weren't talking about just one B-2. Initially, there was to be a squadron of 132 of these bombers, a number that was whittled down to seventy-five and eventually to twenty, although even that figure remained open for discussion.

Once again, the discussion flowed from a bipartisan group that stood together in the face of strong party pressure to stand down. And once again, I was privileged to be a part of that group, although it was a lonely fight at the outset. In the beginning, it was just me and my good friend Ron Dellums, a decidedly liberal black Democrat from Berkeley, California, who would go on to become chairman of the Armed Services Committee. We were an unlikely pair, to throw in together over such as this, but we saw this one issue through a similar lens. Over the next ten years, our opposition effort grew to where our fiscally and patriotically sound arguments became more and more popular, but it wasn't an easy position to take in the early going. Only a few Republicans stood against the defense establishment in those days—and yet there we were, standing for something we all believed was right and good for the future of America.

At one point, Dick Cheney made a side deal with me to freeze the number of planes on order at twenty, in exchange for my agreeing to back down in my fight, which Newt Gingrich and company could then take as my grudging support. We even shook hands on it, and yet a year or so later Cheney was out there thumping for forty. I went onto the House floor and accused him of breaking his word, and to this day he despises me for it, but I felt it was the right thing to do, to call him out in this public way.

We should all be accountable for our actions, wouldn't you agree? Parents, teachers, businessmen and -women . . . and yes, even our government leaders. *Especially* our government leaders. It seemed to me, then and still, that if we are vested with the power to broker deals, and to negotiate with one another for our support of various bills or programs or measures, then we are honor-bound to live up to those agreements, even if they are made on the fly or in some back room or corridor. We ought to be good to our word—because, in the end, that's all we've got. "In God We Trust" . . . it says as much right there on our dollar bills. But what about our government officials? We should have a few more reasons to trust in them as well.

Back to that B-2 fight. For my money, which I tended to see as the American taxpayers' money, I wanted to cancel the plan and redirect some of those funds to develop standoff weapons, a relatively new technology at the time, one that would allow us to accurately fire against our enemies at tremendous distance from our targets. Now, nearly twenty years later, these so-called smart weapons are an essential part of our defense arsenal, and have been put to both cost-effective and tactically effective use, but back then our party was prepared to throw massive amounts into its B-2 program. For a time, many of the major defense contractors and subcontractors in America would have loved to have seen me get hit by a cement truck, that's how incensed people were at my position. Thankfully, I wasn't standing alone. Ron Dellums was right there alongside me, stride for stride, and together we lifted our voices and hoped to start a chorus. We were indeed an unlikely pair, but we became great friends along the way. I'll never forget our very first press conference. There was a reporter from the *Chicago Tribune* and another from the *Columbus Dispatch*, and then there was the two of us, and I remember thinking we were pretty much alone in this fight.

(I also remember thinking we'd need to do a much better job getting support for our position, considering that we couldn't even drag Dellums's hometown paper to our first press conference!)

It was the fight of our political lives. You don't just kill a major weapons system like the B-2 stealth bomber, but that's what we set out to do. We fought the Republicans. We fought the Democrats. We fought every special interest group that took a special interest in the fight. And our hands were tied the whole way. We couldn't give out PAC money. We couldn't fly people out to California to get a look at these planes. It didn't happen overnight, but we got it done. After ten relentless years, during which Ron Dellums and I refused to back down and managed to bring a whole bunch of good people over to our side of the debate, from both sides of the aisle, production was stopped after those twenty planes, and it marked the first time in the twentieth century that a major weapons system had been halted.

ON REFLECTION

For too long in this country, the definition of good politics has been success—meaning how successful you've been in seeking and retaining office—but that's not my definition of good politics, and it certainly isn't my definition of success. To me, good politics is not winning, it's doing. More than that, it's doing the right thing—doing right by your constituents, doing right by your principles, doing right by the values that shaped and defined you as a child. If you win, that's great. If you lose, that's okay, too, as long as you were true to those values, and true to your word, and true to yourself. That, to me, is success. If you don't get elected, you can move on. There are worse things in life than standing for something and losing an election as a result. Life goes on, and there are bigger and better opportunities around every corner. I truly believe that.

By the time I was elected to my final term in Congress in 1998, I could see that the Republicans were faltering. The discipline we had demonstrated on the budget was lost. The ability to seek out our Democratic colleagues and to build consensus on a variety of issues was suddenly beyond our reach. Where there had only recently been a strong sense of purpose and resolve and sacrifice there was once again a vacuum, and this was especially troubling because this was a crowd that had done some great things in my political lifetime. Not only did we balance the budget, but we paid down the largest amount of debt in our nation's history. We saw the dismantling of the Berlin Wall and the Soviet "evil empire." It had been "morning in America," as Ronald Reagan reminded us—and what a wonderful morning it was. And yet without a spirited and inspiriting leader like Reagan to guide us, we had started to give it all back, to where we were once again operating in business-as-usual mode, and I started to think the Founding Fathers had been right to seek a limited government, because at any given time the generally good people who occupy that government are likely to be swayed by so many outside forces and special interests that we'll need to put some checks and balances in place to keep everyone honest.

I also started to think that perhaps I might offer some of that leadership, and so I threw my hat in the ring as a candidate for the Republican presidential nomination in 2000. Recall, it had been one of my childhood dreams to become President of the United States, and here I caught myself thinking that even if my reach happened to exceed my grasp on this one I would do well to reach just the same. Just as it was with my first campaign for the state senate, I didn't have a whole lot of resources, and pundits didn't give me any real shot at winning, but I kept at it for as long as my money held out, and one of the main reasons I held on was because I believed deeply in what I was talking about. I thought I had some pretty good ideas, and I wanted to give them a hearing, but at the same time I didn't want to go into debt. The shocker, to most everyone around me, was that when I announced that I was folding the tent on my presidential campaign, I also announced that I was retiring from Congress. Why? Because I had started to think there just weren't enough hours left in my days for me to accomplish everything I wanted to accomplish in elected office, and that I could perhaps do some of those things more effectively in the private sector. I could stand on the outside looking in, and work to bring about change from a new perspective. Anyway, I thought, I could give it a try.

And then a curious thing happened. I started to realize that no one really remembers you once you leave office. Most politicians don't understand this until they step off the political treadmill and even then we're slow to cop to it. But I recognized that the impact most of us manage to make is no more lasting than a footprint in the sand. Like athletes, our time at the top is short; our legacies, if we managed to build them at all, fade quickly from memory. When the tide comes in, and time marches on, our contributions are all but lost—and all that remains, at best, is a snapshot. I guess I'm mixing my metaphors again on this one, but you get the idea. Politicians have to ask themselves how they want to be remembered, and to accept that they most likely won't be remembered at all. What do we want that snapshot to be? How do I want to answer my daughters when they ask me what I did when I was in office? Do I want to be able to say that I was a good Republican, or a good Democrat, and leave it at that? I don't think so. That's not enough. Not even close.

Ronald Reagan's snapshot? Vision. Strength. Freedom. These are his enduring legacies. In time, no one will remember the Iran-contra scandal, but they'll remember the man and what he stood for. They'll remember JFK's youthful vigor and idealism; Jimmy Carter and the momentary peace in the Middle East, and his humanitarian works since he left office; George W. Bush standing tall and firm amidst the hallowed ashes at Ground Zero. And this is at the big-time level. Most politicians don't get to that big-time level. Most of us have our footprints washed away by the next wave of politicians, and we return to our lives and our families and worry only of the legacy we have left for our children.

C. S. Lewis wrote at length about what he called "the inner ring," and man's constant struggle to be accepted within it, but I'm here to tell you that you can't fight the status quo and still be accepted by an inner circle. And the dirty little secret is that there is no inner circle. It's a mutually exclusive thing, and it gets back to that snapshot. Nobody's going to remember you anyway, so you might as well walk that lonely road and fight that good fight and stand for something and do the right thing.

When I got into politics, it reminded me of all those baseball games I used to go to as a kid. Have you ever noticed how kids go to ballgames wearing the full uniform of their favorite team? Well, that was me. I used to wear my Pirates uniform to Forbes Field. I wore number 21—Roberto Clemente's number—I guess on the thinking that if they ever needed anybody to fill in I'd be ready, and from this perspective being elected to Congress was a lot like getting called onto the field of play at Forbes Field. I made a promise to myself that if I ever got to the plate at Forbes Field I wouldn't bunt. I wouldn't sacrifice. I'd swing for the fences. Every day was an opportunity to do something significant, because I couldn't know how many days I'd have and I didn't want to waste any of them, and I realize that this mind-set runs counter to all those politicians who look at one day merely as a bridge to the next day. It's all about prolonging their time in office, and not at all about making the most of their time in office. It's a fundamental difference. It's about bunting, instead of swinging for the fences. And the folks who play it safe, they're not bad people. After all, it's human nature to want to keep your job and get reelected and be liked and admired by your friends and neighbors back home. Let us never forget that there's a constant pressure to cave in to the status quo. Teachers, lobbyists, senior citizens, NRA-types . . . they're all banging away at you at home. But when the majority is fixed on a noble goal, these pressures can be overcome and good things can happen.

I'll end with a footnote to the story with which I opened this chapter, the one about the well-read woman who cornered me over dinner one night just a few days before the 2004 presidential election, alarmed that the country might not survive its outcome. Remember how she had been all distraught and whipped into uncertainty by political pundits who maintained that the fate of the free world hung in the balance? And, in turn, how I tried to calm her fears by asserting that America would survive, no matter what the outcome of the election? Well, she called me on the Monday night just before the election to thank me for setting her mind at ease.

"I had my first good night's sleep in months," she told me happily, and in her peace of mind I heard the reassurance we'd all do well to take for ourselves.

See, I choose to celebrate the good in people—and, therefore, the good in our systems as well. Our democratic system of government is as good as it gets; its potential lies in great leaders and people back home who demand better; we're blessed to stand on its foundation. Sure, some of us stand a bit taller than others, and quite a few of us get caught stooping to some unimaginable levels, but the abiding strength of our government is that it can reinvent itself. From one generation to the next, or from one election to the next, our system can bend to accommodate the national mood. Today's leaders can be voted out of office at the next opportunity, and they often are when their constituents no longer share their views, or their style. Just because you hold important office today doesn't mean you'll hold that same important office tomorrow. It's what you do with your time in that office that counts—and if it doesn't amount to all that much . . . well, then who's really the poorer for it, after all?

4

TAKING A STAND ON SPORTS

"Unlike any other business in the United States,
sports must preserve an illusion of perfect innocence.
The mounting of this illusion defines the purpose and
accounts for the immense wealth of American sports.
It is the ceremony of innocence that the fans pay to
see—not the game or the match or the bout, but the
ritual portrayal of a world in which time stops and all
hope remains plausible, in which everybody present
can recover the blameless expectations of a child,
where the forces of light always triumph over the
powers of darkness."

Lewis Lapham

Ozzie Guillen, the Venezuelan-born manager of the
2005 World Series champion Chicago White Sox, keeps a sign
on his clubhouse wall, admonishing his players to stand for the

national anthem at the start of each game. It's one of the few hard-and-fast rules in Guillen's relatively loose clubhouse.

The penalty for missing the anthem? A $500 fine—and the unending loss of regard of one of baseball's most outspoken personalities. "If you're not from this country, you should respect the anthem even more than Americans because you should feel pleased you're here," Guillen told *Sports Illustrated* about a month into the 2005 season, explaining his position. "And if you're from this country, you should have respect for people who are dying for it. This is a great country. It has the right of free speech. That's why a lot of countries have problems, because people can't speak for themselves."

Well said.

In the world of sports, Ozzie Guillen stands apart because he stands for something, and he means for his players to stand for something as well—a perspective that contrasts mightily with one of the most disturbing developments from the 2004 baseball season, wherein then–Toronto Blue Jays first baseman and perennial Most Valuable Player candidate Carlos Delgado famously refused to stand for "God Bless America." Delgado, who was born in Puerto Rico and who played for a Canadian team, managed to duck the issue by claiming he had no direct ties to the United States and was therefore not showing any disrespect when he remained in the clubhouse as the song was played during the seventh-inning stretch—and yet Americans were right to feel dissed.

At the time, Delgado claimed his refusal was a protest of the war in Iraq, which he called "the stupidest war ever." Regrettably, Delgado's position ran somewhat counter to his other claim, that he had no real stake in American affairs, and I think people responded to the hypocrisy. Delgado himself must have sensed that public sentiment was against him, because when he became a free agent following the 2004 season and peddled his services to the highest bidder, he made a special point of promising to stand for the anthem out of respect for his new employers and his new hometown fans. Unofficially, it marked the first time a baseball player's pledge of allegiance to the United States was used as a negotiating ploy, and for my money it also marked a new low in the declining standards to which we hold our professional athletes. And Delgado promptly lived down to our low expectations; he quickly signed a four-year, $52 million contract with the Florida Marlins, after which he let slip that now that he had gotten what he wanted he wasn't sure he would stand for the anthem after all.

Like millions of American baseball fans, I was so disgusted by Delgado's tactics that I can no longer root for him, but I can't honestly say I was surprised. We've come to demand so little of our professional athletes off the field of play it's a wonder we continue to cast them as role models for our children, and lately their churlish behavior has found its way onto the field as well, to where I find myself thinking that Ozzie Guillen is someone I want on my team while Carlos Delgado emerges as someone I want to run out of town.

Consider these recent *lowlights* from the world of sports and you'll get what I mean:

• *Latrell Sprewell, the onetime National Basketball Association all-star guard, alienated fans and foes alike when he criticized Minnesota Timberwolves management for not extending his contract before the start of the 2004–2005 season, for which he would be paid*

$14.6 million. "Why would I want to help them win a title?" he told reporters, with the arrogance folks had come to expect from a player who once choked his coach. "They're not doing anything for me. I'm at risk. I have a lot of risk here. I got my family to feed." And the most galling piece to Sprewell's insensitive cry of poverty was that he wasn't the first wildly overpaid NBA superstar to suggest he'd completely lost touch with the average fan who somehow manages to come up with close to $100 per ticket for the privilege of watching these louts play. Once, during a 1999 work stoppage, New York Knicks center Patrick Ewing begged public sympathy by suggesting that folks need to understand the unique financial circumstance of professional athletes. "We make a lot of money," he said. "But we spend a lot of money, too."

• Notre Dame head football coach George O'Leary was fired after only five days on the job, after it was discovered that he had lied on his résumé. The scandal rocked the college football powerhouse, and prompted some die-hard Fighting Irish fans to whine that lying on résumés was a fact of American life, and that O'Leary's subsequent accomplishments as head football coach at Georgia Tech should have superseded his relatively inconsequential résumé padding. O'Leary himself protested the decision by pointing to his considerable credentials, and suggested that the lies on his résumé were no big deal. Clearly, his record of achievement didn't need any embellishment, but what O'Leary and his supporters didn't understand was that college football coaches ought to be held to a higher standard than their players or boosters.

• Randy Moss, the talented wide receiver now toiling for the Oakland Raiders of the National Football League, justified his increasingly vulgar (and hardly spontaneous) "touchdown dances" to celebrate his end zone catches by claiming that the only consequence to his actions was a fine levied by the league. "Ain't nothing but ten grand," he said, *after pretending to drop his pants and moon the Green Bay crowd in a January 2005 playoff game while he was a member of the Minnesota Vikings. "What's ten grand to me?" Moss's agent, Dante DiTrapano, however, argued that the fine was extravagant and unnecessary and planned to appeal. "If you can't have freedom of expression on the football field, come on," the agent said. Moss's coach, Mike Tice, maintained that he didn't see Moss's boorish behavior and could therefore not comment on it, which I guess amounts to looking the other way. (And it seems to ignore the obvious fact of videotape, and that he could have screened his receiver's antics from every conceivable angle following the game.) For his part, Moss demonstrated a remarkable inability to gauge public opinion and promised that his next end zone celebrations would be even more offensive.*

• University of Miami officials poked additional holes in the confused notion that student athletes can do no wrong by admitting highly recruited high school linebacker Willie Williams, after it was revealed that he had been arrested eleven times in the previous five years. The revelations came to light after a recruiting visit to the Miami campus the previous spring. "Just to decline a recommendation to admit a player because of what somebody might think nationally, I just don't think that is the right way to handle it," said Hurricanes coach Larry Coker in defending the university's decision. School officials contended that they were not aware of Williams's criminal history when he accepted Miami's scholarship offer.

And so I'll ask what sometimes strikes me as the defining question of our times: What the heck is going on here? And, more to the point, when did we get so accustomed on a societal level to the bad behavior, bad judgment, and bad examples of our big-time athletes or our big-time athletic programs that it started to roll off us like nothing much at all? When did the bar of expectations fall so low that an ant could clear it without too much effort? And why does it all seem to matter—more so now than at any other time in our recent history?

Well, from the beginning of recorded civilization, athletic competition has been a kind of societal proving ground. What are the Olympic games, after all, but an extension of an ancient ritual to honor our best athletes, and to bestow upon them the riches and virtues and accolades we might otherwise seek for ourselves? The struggle to succeed in sports mirrors our struggle to succeed in our workaday world, and each reinforces the notion that if you work hard, dream big, and play as a team good things will come your way.

WHY SPORTS MATTERS

World-class athletes, by their grace and dedication and prowess, are the physical manifestation of our shared quest for excellence. They have incredible gifts, and their success brings them money, fame, and glory. The twenty-four-hour media attention that comes their way as a result also gives them a tremendous responsibility to model behavior that is consistent with their work ethic on the field of play, and yet in recent years athletes have been dropping the ball in this one area at an alarming rate. Think back to the inspiring examples of Jesse Owens, who used his powerful body to combat Nazi propaganda during World War Two; Sandy Koufax, who followed his faith and refused to participate in a baseball game that might have decided a championship because it fell on one of the holiest days of the Jewish calendar; Arnold Palmer, whose tremendous humility has won

him an army of fans, even as his dominance set him a couple fair-
ways apart from his competitors; Jim Abbott, the left-handed
pitcher who overcame enormous physical disabilities to enjoy a
remarkable major league career that included a no-hitter for the
New York Yankees. Think back to the superstar athletes of yes-
teryear and wonder when it was we started expecting *less* of our
heroes—and, as a result, receiving less in return.

To be sure, we spend so much time worshipping celebrities in
this society that when we cast these athletes in the same role we
start to think they can do no wrong. (And—even worse—*they*
move about thinking the same!) Deserving or not, athletes are
role models to our children, and we need to get wise to the
learned truths that they *can* do wrong, that they very often do,
and that the nature of these wrongs can have profound implications. Still, even our best athletes can fade quickly from memory;
their time at the top is short; with each succeeding generation
there will always be someone faster, stronger, and more talented
ready to take the helm. And yet because we invest our star athletes with such formative influence, and allow them to stand as
role models for our children, their legacies can live on long after
they leave their games behind.

Consider: John McEnroe starts throwing his tennis racket and
ranting and raving at fans and officials, and soon enough there
are thousands of John McEnroe wannabes, throwing their tennis
rackets on their neighborhood courts and kicking up the kind of
fuss that in my day would have earned a licking.

Baseball players juice themselves with steroids so they can hit
more home runs, and before long high school players are roam-
ing the nutritional supplement aisles at the drugstore looking for
the same edge.

Football players taunt their opponents after a sack and the next thing you know you've got kids in Pop Warner and Pee Wee leagues all around the country trash talking and piling on.

U.S. figure skater Tonya Harding notoriously engages a hit man to take a blunt object to the knee of her American teammate Nancy Kerrigan, the reigning national champion and Harding's chief rival for a gold medal at the 1994 Winter Olympics in Norway—sending a powerful message to young athletes all over the world that if you can't beat 'em in head-to-head competition it's sometimes okay to beat 'em with a blunt object instead and avoid the athletic confrontation entirely.

Of course, there are wonderful exceptions to the general decline in sportsmanship and leadership. There's cyclist Lance Armstrong, setting new standards in one of the world's most grueling competitions and at the same time calling important attention to the struggle with cancer that he shares with millions worldwide. There's legally blind musher Rachel Scdoris, who thrillingly completed the 1,200-mile Iditarod dog sled race and sent a powerful message to disabled individuals that anything was possible. There's tennis great Andre Agassi, who donated millions to establish a charter school in an impoverished section of his hometown, returning something in a bricks-and-mortar way to the community that helped shape him.

But these are the exceptions in a generally self-centered field of superstars. Our most gifted athletes are coddled at such a young age they get to thinking they're held to a different standard than the rest of us—which too often means no standard at all. There's no discipline, no consequences, and so they slip through the system believing that the rules of polite society don't apply to them. At the same time, they look on at their own so-called heroes, and start modeling their behavior on the back of these bad examples. It all feeds on itself, and the further along they get in their athletic development, the more deeply ingrained these negative traits become. They don't know any other way.

That's the nut of it, really, that we invest these superstar athletes with far too much influence. It's a huge responsibility, to set a positive example every time you leave the house, every time you step to the plate, every time you're out on the town following a game, and too many of these young stars are just not up to it. Even the veterans find it tough to be under such a constant spotlight, and most coaches don't have the first idea how to rein these guys in. Coaches have a hard enough time getting athletes to demonstrate leadership on the field and in the clubhouse, and when it comes to demonstrating leadership off the field they'll take the position that it's not in their contract.

We also cut them way too much slack, wouldn't you agree? Lately, our police blotters are filled with the names of star athletes commanding special treatment on account of their celebrity. Fleet-footed shortstop Rafael Furcal was allowed to play in the 2004 Major League Baseball playoffs for the Atlanta Braves despite a drunk driving conviction that would have landed most of us directly in jail. I mentioned this story earlier, but it deserves another nod here as one of the most disgraceful headlines in recent memory. "I don't know what the Braves would do without him," Furcal's attorney told a state court judge, who was either a fan or a fool because he put sentencing on hold until Atlanta completed its playoff run.

Baltimore Ravens running back Jamal Lewis pleaded guilty to

drug charges just prior to the start of the 2004 season, but was allowed to schedule his prison term at the end of the NFL season.

Even synchronized swimmer Tammy Crow was free to participate in the 2004 Summer Olympics in Athens after being convicted of vehicular manslaughter, before beginning her three-month sentence a few days after the closing ceremonies. Here again, the disgrace runs to all of us, for placing these athletes on such a pedestal that even a bronze medal in synchronized swimming counts for something beyond a deserved punishment meted out in a timely fashion.

A DIFFERENT STANDARD

Apparently, when athletes get together to talk about the fringe benefits of sports, the benefit of the doubt must rank pretty high on their list, because these examples of slippery justice just go on and on. I don't mean to suggest that every athlete who winds up facing charges gets a lighter sentence than anonymous individuals facing the same charges, or that they get to schedule their prison terms whenever it's most convenient, but there's a pattern here, and an undeniable connection between the athlete who grows up under the silver lining of preferential treatment and second chances and the belligerent professional who is so emboldened by his fame and fortune that he just can't help himself. At some point, we have to take some of the responsibility for all this on our own shoulders, because we're the ones letting these athletes off the hook. We're the ones setting this new standard, because by looking the other way from all this bad behavior, or reducing or rescheduling their justified punishments, we're really just encouraging more of the same.

Just look at Major League Baseball's policy on steroids, which has lately commanded front and center attention in baseball circles and in Congress. In one respect, the league's message is clear: Steroids are illegal, and dangerous, and irresponsible, and those who take them are gaining an unfair competitive advantage that threatens not only their health but also the health of impressionable young athletes who model their training and conditioning after their favorite ballplayers. They threaten the integrity of the game. And yet in another respect, the message has until recently been mixed, because a player needed to get caught five times before he could be thrown out of the league for taking these banned substances. Five times! Where else but in the arena of professional sports does an individual get five strikes before he gets what's coming to him? Apparently owners and players have responded to public sentiment on this one and have agreed to tougher penalties for steroid use beginning with the 2006 baseball season, penalties that include a 50-game suspension for the first offense, 100 games for the second, and a lifetime ban for the third.

Mercifully, there have been some other hopeful developments regarding athletes and the coaches and agents and university officials charged with their safekeeping. It's not all shock and awe out there. In fact, the only good thing about this never-ending *lowlight* reel from the world of sports is that it sets us up for the *highlights* that find us every time an Ozzie Guillen or Lance Armstrong alights on our radar. One of the happiest surprises to emerge from the world of sports in 2005 was the principled stand taken by Bill Brogden, the men's golf coach at Tulsa, during a sudden-death playoff with SMU to decide the Western Athletic Conference championship. The two teams were playing a course in Choudrant, Louisiana, about a half-hour from the nearest airport, and as the day drew long Coach Brogden realized he was getting perilously close to his team's scheduled departure for the last flight of the day to take them home.

The playoff format meant it would be at least another hour before a winner would be decided, and by that point the team's plane would be on the tarmac, awaiting takeoff. Coach Brogden knew full well that three of his five players had final exams first thing the next morning, and that four of them maintained grade point averages of 3.2 or above, and that he couldn't afford to let them miss that plane, title on the line or no. So what did he do? He conceded the championship by forfeit and made certain his players were on the last flight out of town. How about that? In a world where winning at all costs is too often prized above else, Coach Brogden let it be known that some things were more important than winning. Surprised the heck out of his own administration, too, so much so that the president of the university sent a memo to every faculty member at the school, in which he indicated that he had never been more proud of a coach or a team, and that Coach Brodgen's decision "shines brighter than any trophy."

Yes it does.

Sometimes, the shining examples hit closer to home. Consider the recent choices made by the Miami Dolphins' Tebucky Jones, who woke up one day and realized his three kids—with their Xboxes and iPods and Abercrombie & Fitch wardrobes—had it a little too soft, especially compared to his own hardscrabble upbringing. Realize, Tebucky Jones had it pretty rough as a kid growing up in New Britain, Connecticut. His family was evicted twenty-three times before he got out of high school. He kept warm in his unheated apartment by sticking a lit match in a mayonnaise jar. He got a girl pregnant when he was just fourteen years old.

That he ended up marrying the girl, and going on to become one of the NFL's brightest stars, didn't change his backstory, and yet his own children never knew what it meant to struggle. They can still remember the day their dad's $2.65 million signing bonus arrived in the mail, after he was made a first-round draft choice of the New England Patriots in 1998, and it seemed like all the money in the world because it was. Just a few years earlier, living up in Syracuse, their father didn't even have enough money to buy them a Christmas tree, and all of a sudden he was rolling in it.

"I wanted them to know how lucky they were, that when I told them stories about my life it wasn't bull," Jones told *ESPN: The Magazine*. "A lot of kids are snobs. But I wanted them to know we're all human. I wanted them to see both sides of life."

So what did Jones do? He piled his kids into his fancy car, drove them back to his hometown, and dropped them off at the curb in front of the Boys and Girls Club—the same club he went to when he was a kid. Not much had changed over the years, and his pampered kids stood out like the rich kids they were, but Jones pulled away and left them to their own devices. The following week, they returned to the club. And the week after that. And the week after that. It took a while, but his children began to develop a tougher exterior, and a fuller appreciation for the world around. They watched each other's backs, and helped each other grow. Jones wanted them to learn to take care of themselves, to value what they had, to gain some much needed perspective, and he knew enough to realize it wouldn't come by words alone.

And what about Pat Tillman, the Arizona Cardinals football player who walked away from a $1.2 million professional contract to enlist in the U.S. Army Rangers shortly after September 11, 2001? This was a guy who had a standout college career at Arizona State, and who was a starter at the professional level, but he was largely unknown outside Arizona until he decided his place was in the military, where he could fight for his country. Folks across the country responded to his decision as if they'd never heard of such a thing—a professional athlete walking away from a lucrative contract in the prime of his career to fight for the U.S. Army because he believed it was the right thing to do, the only thing to do. Tillman's reputation grew when he returned home from his initial tour in Iraq and decided to reup for a second tour instead of seeking his discharge and returning to professional football, because he felt strongly that some things were more important than professional football. Four months later, on April 22, 2004, he was shot and killed in Afghanistan, leaving behind a legacy of selfless leadership without peer among contemporary athletes.

Pat Tillman also left behind a legion of friends, in the world of football and beyond; actually, he made such an impact that the NFL decided to honor his memory by having all players wear a decal with Tillman's number—40—on their helmets during one week of league play. One player, Tillman's former Arizona State roommate Jake Plummer, who was now playing quarterback for the Denver Broncos, was so moved by the tribute that he wore the decal again the following week, only this time the league didn't think this was such a good idea. Plummer was fined

$10,000, for donning an item not covered in the league's elaborate uniform code, which prohibits the display of personal messages on uniforms and helmets, and warned that the fine would double each time out, which struck me as one of the most absurd rulings I'd ever heard—especially since the very decal had been designed by the league and authorized for just this purpose for games played the week before. Plummer didn't know what to do, and thought initially that the best way to memorialize his fallen friend was to play by the rules, so he peeled the decal off his helmet for the next game. The following week, he put it back on, and I looked on at home and cheered. Fans across the country must have done the same, because hundreds of them pledged to pay the fines if they were ever assessed—and when they were, Plummer asked the NFL, which donates fines to charity, to give the money to the Pat Tillman Foundation.

As long as I'm on it, how goofy is it that the league itself, which already has an image problem with so many players facing criminal charges for dubious conduct off the field, and so many more facing public disapproval for dubious conduct on the field, calls an upstanding guy like Jake Plummer to task for doing something that most of us regard as moral, and right, and true? Makes you wonder what these people are thinking.

Then there's high school basketball coach Ken Carter, who once padlocked the gymnasium doors at Richmond High in northern California because nearly half his players were ditching their classes, and who suspended practices and forfeited all his team's games until his players improved their grades. Next, Coach Carter made his players sign contracts promising to sit in the front row of their classes and maintain grade point averages a full grade higher than the state-mandated minimum for student athletes. His players had to call him "sir," and they had to wear coats and ties to school on game days, and pitch in around the school on various fund-raising and cleanup efforts. They were expected to be model citizens, or they would be cut from the team. He taught them that instead of dreaming of becoming the next Michael Jordan, they'd do well to be the guy who signs the next Michael Jordan's paycheck. He commanded respect, and he gave it in return, and I can't shake wondering why we don't see more Coach Carters celebrated in our sports pages.

His methods weren't all that popular at first, but Coach Carter struck such a chord with his players and his community that Hollywood producers turned his experiences into a recent movie, *Coach Carter*, starring Samuel L. Jackson. "What I want people to take from this movie is that respect, self-discipline, and being kind will never, ever go out of style," Carter told the *New York Times* upon the movie's release.

No, Coach, they won't—but we will lose sight of them from time to time, particularly on and around our playing fields. See, this win-at-all-costs mind-set has permeated the culture to such an alarming degree that a tossed-off rallying cry once attributed to legendary football coach Vince Lombardi has become a justification for just about anything: "Winning isn't everything, it's the only thing." Nothing against Lombardi, whose words might have been a powerful motivational tool when shouted out in a locker room full of professional athletes, but they carry a different message as the phrase takes root in the culture, don't you think? I hear that phrase, out of context, and I think we've lost our sense of place and purpose. I hear that phrase and I get these feelings of outrage, at the way we've allowed these gifted young men and women to poison our shared notion of right and wrong, or the ways our university athletic directors have pushed student athletes to value their points-per-game average over their grade point average, and if I'm being completely honest I'll allow that a good chunk of that outrage is directed at myself. Let's face it, I'm like most people I know—in business, in politics, in the world. I'm competitive. I like to win. Why? Well, it's a whole lot more fun than losing, and it opens many more doors besides. It's thrilling, and validating, and in many ways it justifies the point of the whole darn enterprise, whatever it happens to be. Plus, I don't much see the point in running a campaign, say, if you've got no hope of winning, or going through the motions on a particular project just to see a thing through. Sure, I can recognize the value in doing something well, simply for the sake of doing it, but we're conditioned to think there's an endgame to everything. Something has got to be at stake to make it all worthwhile.

I catch myself thinking this way, but then I think of my daughters, and the lessons I want them to take away from each and every day. Do I really want them to go to a high school where the phrase "winning is the only thing" might hang on a banner from the gymnasium ceiling? Once again, this is not a rap on Lombardi, who by all accounts was an inspiration to his players and a stand-up guy, but I don't think so. Granted, my daughters are just starting kindergarten, but I fast-forward their little lives to where I can layer what I know onto the young women they will too soon become, and I don't always like where they appear headed. I don't like what lies in wait. I don't like the cultural indicators that will be in place as they get older to help them discover right from wrong, and I particularly don't like the ones that might flow from the world of sports, because they're shot through with so many mixed messages that even we caring, well-meaning adults sometimes have trouble figuring them out.

THE PRICE OF WINNING

I'll tell a story on myself, to illustrate just how much I want to win, and just how much that wanting to win can sometimes get in the way of my better judgment. I think we all struggle with this dichotomy, to a degree, and the key here is to pay attention to these base impulses and do what we can to keep them in check. Here's what happened: I was playing golf with a group of friends. We take our golf seriously. There's money on the line, but it's not a great deal of money, and whatever the amount it doesn't come close to the ego that's involved. It's a pride thing, with our group, a bragging rights thing, more than it is a money thing, and it was beneath the cloud of this type of thinking that I approached my ball on the fairway this one afternoon. I'd been playing well, the bragging rights were within reach, and then I shanked a shot. Happens all the time to us duffers, right? So I told the caddie to chase down that first ball while I hit another one, and after I drove this second shot onto the green I realized none of my buddies had seen my first shot, and for a moment in there I got so completely caught up in this warped, win-at-all-costs mentality that gets some of these athletes and coaches into so much trouble that I wasn't thinking all that straight.

I walked to the green and putted out, and as I reached down to pick up my ball I thought to myself, What am I doing here? This was supposed to be a game. These were supposed to be my friends. And besides, I realized, the caddie had seen that first shot. Heck, he chased down the ball for me and returned it to my bag. And yet there I was, thinking about taking a five on the hole instead of the six I deserved, and I couldn't for the life of me understand why. For a couple beats in there, I didn't quite know how to play it, as my buddy with the scorecard crossed over to me and said, "That's a five, isn't it?"

I froze. It was just a split second or so, but in my mind it was an eternity, until I finally said, "No, it was a six."

"What do you mean, a six?" my buddy shot back.

I said, "Well, I missed a shot."

It would have never in a million years occurred to this guy that I was thinking of shaving that mulligan off my score, even for just that split second, and even as I write this I'm wondering why I'm copping to it here, but I think it reinforces an all-important point. We're human. We can't help ourselves. *I'm* human. *I* can't help myself. And yet, with reflection, most of us manage to get it right, most of the time.

After I put in my score, I crossed over to my caddie and said, "I want you to know, I recorded a six on that hole."

He nodded, like he expected nothing less, and in the exchange I wondered what kind of leader I would be if I let this guy go home thinking I had cheated my friends out of that one stroke. What would my daughters have thought, if they'd been watching? It goes back to that daddy-cam notion I wrote about in my opening remarks, the concept of living each day as if our children are watching—because they are. All the time. And there's a record button built into the thing, too, because our kids will replay our missteps over and over and over again.

What we all need to recognize is that it's not just the players. The bad behavior has spilled into the stands as well, while the bad judgment has reached all the way to the front office. One of the most horrifying stories to emerge in the months surrounding the writing of this book was the bench-clearing brawl that erupted between the Indiana Pacers and the Detroit Pistons during the opening weeks of the 2004–2005 NBA season—and it was horrifying at every level of the game. Players, fans, management . . . they were all out of line, as I will attempt to explain. If you were anywhere near a television during the week of November 19, 2004, you probably saw some of the footage, because it was played over and over on every network and cable news channel. The fight itself was bad enough, but it appeared to have been jump-started by a Detroit fan who must have thought his ticket to the game at the Palace of Auburn Hills entitled him also to dump a cup of beer on the Pacers' Ron Artest, who happened to be stretched out on the scorer's table while officials attempted to sort out the worst offenders from the preliminary round of the fight.

(How about setting our daddy-cam on *that* guy, and letting his kids rethink their opinion of him?)

What happened next was almost surreal, as players on both teams began trading punches with fans in the stands and on the floor. Clearly, the idiot fan should have never doused an opposing player with beer, and the other idiot fans should have never started throwing punches, or taunting the players in any way, but the players should have never returned the blows; they should have walked away and left it to security officials to sort out the mess, but of course that could have never happened, because these athletes had been conditioned since childhood to give as good as they got; they would not be disrespected; they would not stand down.

FAR-REACHING CONSEQUENCES—OR JUST A BAD BREAK?

When the dust cleared, NBA commissioner David Stern handed down suspensions to eight players involved in the fighting, with the most severe penalties going to Indiana's Ron Artest, who was suspended for the balance of the season, Stephen Jackson, who was suspended for thirty games, and Jermaine O'Neal, who was suspended for twenty-five games.

"The actions of the players involved wildly exceeded the professionalism and self-control that should fairly be expected from NBA players," Stern stated at his press conference to announce the suspensions. "We must affirm that the NBA will strive to exemplify the best that can be offered by professional sports and not allow our sport to be debased by what seem to be declining expectations for the behavior of fans and athletes alike."

Like the brawl itself, Stern's press conference received wide media attention, but the backroom appeals from the NBA players' association were given scant notice by comparison—and for some reason this last struck me as perhaps the most disturbing part of the whole imbroglio. When a federal judge granted a request to halt O'Neal's twenty-five-game suspension at just fifteen games, the news was cause for celebration in Indianapolis, where the hometown Pacers had been struggling without their star player. Pacers president Donnie Walsh, an educated man and a purported community leader who should have known better, led the cheers. "It's a great jolt at a time when we need it," he said.

What an affront, I thought when I heard Walsh's remarks, and what a poor excuse for leadership, to welcome a disgraced player like O'Neal back into the fold simply in the name of winning. O'Neal had served just 60 percent of Stern's original sentence, and here was his employer, publicly rejoicing that a Get Out of Jail Free card had been played in his name and his team could finally get back to playing at something close to full strength.

Certainly, O'Neal's behavior on November 19, 2004, was despicable, but if I was president of the Indiana Pacers, I would have considered weighing in with even stiffer penalties than the ones levied by the league. In some ways, just to cross sports and toss out a baseball metaphor to make a point, it's as if a player was called out on strikes and then hired an attorney to appeal, arguing that he was denied an opportunity to earn a living by smacking the heck out of the ball and that he should therefore be entitled to another couple swings. That's basically what it came down to. David Stern, who sets the rules and the tone for the entire league, determined what the penalties would be in this case, the players' association argued that the suspension was not in Jermaine O'Neal's best interests, and Donnie Walsh was only too happy to benefit from the reduced sentence. What kind of example does that set? What kind of message does it send to our young people? Donnie Walsh was handed a great opportunity to take some kind of stand, but he took no stand at all, choosing instead to focus on winning over doing the right thing, and it struck me as one of the most cowardly acts I'd seen in sports—or anywhere else for that matter.

And let's not delude ourselves into thinking Walsh's actions in response to his players' behavior didn't resonate with our young athletes. This stuff doesn't happen in a vacuum. The Pistons–Pacers brawl led to dozens of copycat brawls in college, high school, and recreational league gymnasiums across the country— I guess on the confused thinking that if such bad behavior was tolerated at the highest levels of the game it would be tolerated across the board. One such rumble, at a high school girls basketball game in Akron, Ohio, involved players and fans, and resulted in year-long suspensions and criminal charges, as the Ohio High School Athletic Association swiftly established strict penalties for players who climb into the stands to fight with spectators.

I'm afraid this type of executive misstep doesn't end with Donnie Walsh. Even Gary Bettman, the forthright commissioner of the National Hockey League and a man who's been generally admired for his principled stands in the ongoing battle between players and management, made a similar miscalculation when he reinstated an all-star player named Todd Bertuzzi, who had taken out an opposing player named Steve Moore in such a violent and flagrant way that it remained to be seen at the time of Bettman's decision if Moore would ever skate again. Here's what happened on this score: Bertuzzi, playing for the Vancouver Canucks, sucker-punched the Colorado Avalanche's Moore from behind in a March 8, 2004, regular season game, and slammed him face-first onto the ice, breaking Moore's neck. Bertuzzi, widely regarded as one of the best players in the game, was banned from the NHL for the remainder of the 2003–2004 season, and he was due to be suspended indefinitely into the 2004–2005 season as well. I have no issue with the initial punishment, which all concerned seemed to agree was a fair and just response to Bertuzzi's unfair and unjust tactics, but as readers by now know *all* NHL players were effectively suspended for the 2004–2005 season, due to a lockout over a collective bargaining dispute.

As it happened, then, Bertuzzi was forced to sit out only thirteen regular season games, and seven playoff games, resulting in the forfeiture of $501,926.39 in salary—a stiff penalty, to be sure, but one that hardly fit the crime, or the intent of the initial punishment, because in August 2005, Bettman decided to reinstate Bertuzzi, and to treat the lockout season as "time served" on his sentence. Once again, it was an outrage wrapped inside a loophole, and I looked on and thought, Come on, people, let's get together on this one. Realize, as far as the 2004–2005 season was concerned, the man's entire peer group served the same sentence on the sidelines—and none of them had blindsided their opponent and bashed his face onto the ice.

But Bettman didn't see it that way. "From an NHL standpoint," he announced in his prepared statement explaining his decision, "there is no question that Mr. Bertuzzi's actions clearly went well beyond what could ever be considered acceptable behavior in the National Hockey League. Mr. Bertuzzi must be held responsible for the results of his actions, and the message must be delivered loudly and forcefully that the game will not tolerate this type of conduct. I believe that the League's response at the time of the incident and subsequently is consistent with that responsibility and delivers that message." Bettman went on to suggest that Bertuzzi's total suspension reached to nearly seventeen months—"the longest in NHL history"—once again failing to take into account that for most of those seventeen months every NHL player was also suspended due to a league-wide work stoppage.

I'm sorry, but the only message that was delivered loudly and forcefully here is that the owners and executives of our professional sports franchises continue to hold their star players to all kinds of different standards. Apparently, the sight of a run-of-the-mill NHL player lying unconscious in a pool of his own blood is not enough to convince the commissioner that strong leadership is what it will take to stem the rush of bad behavior on our public stages—and to keep our children from beating the tar out of each other just to keep pace with their favorite sports heroes.

It's like one of those societal viruses, this bad behavior, and it's spreading like nobody's business, all because of an alarming lack of leadership. Sure, we can find these little pockets of hope, every here and there, but in general terms things are out of control. We are out of control, and instead of cheering on these knuckleheads from the stands, and buying the sneakers and sportswear and energy drinks they endorse, we should be aligning ourselves with the programs that ratify the principles that resonate at home.

Coaches are standing behind the bums on their rosters like never before—at a time when they should be making examples of them. Why is it that those who follow sports revere a coach like John Wooden, who ruled over UCLA's basketball program for decades with an iron fist and a firm set of rules? Why is it that Vince Lombardi stands so tall in our collective memories? It's because these guys didn't cut any corners, or cut their players any slack. They had discipline. They were principled. They stood for something—and there's nothing more rewarding than to stand for something and to stick to your principles and still be successful.

Nowadays, at the professional level, I look at a guy like Bill Belichick, coach of the New England Patriots of the NFL, and wonder where we might find a couple dozen more just like him. You don't see his players strutting in the end zone, doing these vulgar or taunting dances, or spiking the ball like children. There's none of that arrogant posturing you see around the league. His players just get it done, without calling attention to the doing, and it's a striking thing to see. Mainly, it's the contrast that I find so striking, the way he treats his players as a team instead of as individuals; the way he demands respect and gives it in return; the way his standards are absolute.

The leader sets the tone, and from my sideline perspective it seems Belichick's message is that football is important, and winning is important, but life is more important still. At the end of your days, you're not going to content yourself by counting your Super Bowl rings. You're going to ask yourself, Was I a good person? Did I do the best I could with what I had? Did I treat people the way I wanted to be treated in return? These are the questions for a lifetime, and we draw strength and comfort when the answers come back in the affirmative. After all, as the Bible says, it doesn't pay to inherit the world—or the Super Bowl, or the seven-figure contract—if in the process we lose our character.

Stand for something? You better believe it, only here it means we must decide which teams we want to root for, which athletes we want on our side, which examples we'll let stand for our children.

5

TAKING A STAND
ON BUSINESS

"A business that makes nothing but money is a poor kind of business."

Henry Ford

I'll go out on a limb on this one and state that most businessmen and women are ethical, diligent, conscientious, and driven to succeed. And it had better be a strong limb, because the business sections of our major newspapers are littered with news of one corporate misstep after another. Fraud. Corruption. Inflated earnings. False filings . . . it's enough to leave hardworking Americans wondering where the profit is in an honest day's work.

Taken together, the seemingly endless string of scandals rocking the business world has created an atmosphere of mistrust and disillusion that threatens to quash our spirit of entrepreneurship and kill our willingness to invest in new ideas. It's also threatening to distort the image of corporate America into one that is motivated by greed and avarice instead of one that rises to meet new challenges and pulses to creativity and innovation. How have we allowed this to happen? When did this shift take place? What can we do to clear some of that air and set things right? And, most important, how can we align ourselves with the "right" team and stand against those who give business a bad name?

To begin, we'll need to take a step back and look at the problem through a more forgiving lens, because I honestly believe we've let a relatively few rotten apples spoil the entire barrel on this one. Here's why: The old saw about what makes a good news story holds especially true when it comes to corporate America. It's the same dog-bites-man/man-bites-dog dilemma that has confronted newspaper editors since the invention of movable type. If a local man gets bitten by a local dog, it doesn't make the paper, but if a local man bites a local dog . . . well, that's a lead story. Journalists are not exactly climbing all over themselves to report on the largesse of Bill Gates, who along with his wife, Melinda, has donated more than $28 billion to various charities, including $750 million to the Global Alliance for Vaccines and Immunization and $1 billion toward the establishment of a scholarship program that bears their name; and we can read hardly a word about the good public works of Pierre M. Omidyar, the founder of eBay, who has pledged to give away much of his eBay holdings, estimated to be about $6 billion, to community-based causes that promote activism and volunteerism, including $100 million to his alma mater, Tufts University, for an innovative program to promote social entrepreneurship around the world. After all, if our parents taught us right, inviting others to share in our good fortune is merely what's expected of us. That's not news. It's when we stray from those shared values and expectations that we have a story—and I'm sorry to report there's been a whole lot of straying going on.

STOP THE PRESSES

As I write this, the American business community is struggling to make sense of the latest bulletin to capture media attention—allegations that Wal-Mart's former vice chairman Thomas Coughlin misused up to $500,000 in corporate funds by misappropriating Wal-Mart gift cards for his personal use and filing fraudulent invoices for personal services from third-party vendors—many of these in apparent support of anti-union activities. Granted, on the big-time corporate level, $500,000 is often dismissed as petty cash, but the charges against Coughlin caused a stir precisely because of the relatively low dollar amount involved. Numbers that "small" get tossed aside like nothing at all, when in truth they're "nickel-and-diming" us into confusion. If you're like me, you read about some of these "inside" abuses of power and privilege, by people of stature like Thomas Coughlin, and they're a full-in-the-face reminder how tempting it can be for some of our top executives to cheat both the system and their shareholders, and if it can happen at the hands of one of Sam Walton's last remaining protégés on the board then it can happen anywhere. How is it possible that a guy with all that money, and all that power, is driven to something like this? If the allegations against Coughlin are true, what does it say about the risk-reward model he had in place on this one, that he put everything on the line—career, reputation, family, future—over a relative pittance? What a miscalculation!

In business, as in anything else, timing is everything, and here Thomas Coughlin's apparent bad timing took another bite out of the tanned hide of corporate America. Man bites dog? Heck, it's more like man bites *man*, and when that happens you might as well stop the presses.

Throw this scandal into the mixer with dozens of other high-profile corporate scandals and it adds heat to an already hot debate on the decline of ethics in the business community, and I don't care which side you take up in the argument, you won't be running out of ammunition anytime soon. Consider these recent falls from grace, played out on the front pages of newspapers across the country: John Rigas, chief executive of Adelphia Communications, was found guilty of conspiracy and fraud, for looting as much as $100 million in company funds; Dennis Kozlowski, of Tyco, was found guilty on 22 of 23 counts of grand larceny and conspiracy, having, among other things, diverted company funds to his personal account and thrown a $2 million party on Sardinia for his wife (he was sentenced to 8½ to 25 years in prison and fined $70 million); and Tomo Razmilovic, of Symbol Technologies, fled the country after being charged with securities fraud.

You'll note here that I haven't offered the findings in all of these cases after they went to trial, because many of them remain open at the time of this writing, and in certain cases where the verdicts have come in they have been swiftly appealed, but it's the vast sweep of all these allegations that has gotten me worried. It's the appearance of impropriety—all at once, and all over the corporate map. It's enough to make you question the legitimacy of almost every transaction, without even taking into account the devastating collapses of Enron and WorldCom—two high-flying corporate giants of the middle 1990s booms whose names have now become synonymous with greed and graft and corruption.

In case you missed it—although I can't imagine how—the Enron debacle was a doozy, at the time the largest, most far-reaching accounting fraud and bankruptcy filing in U.S. history. The company grew out of a 1985 merger negotiated by Houston Natural Gas CEO Kenneth Lay, and was originally involved in the transmission and distribution of electricity and gas, and the development and operation of power plants and pipelines around the world. Under Lay's putatively "visionary" direction, it was named "America's Most Innovative Company" by *Fortune* magazine for five consecutive years, from 1996 to 2000, but it was all too good to be true. There were soon charges of irregular accounting procedures bordering on fraud, against Enron and its accounting firm, Arthur Andersen. Here again, the appearance of impropriety set people off, and investigators began looking closely at the company's entire operation. Every day, it seemed, there were new allegations against Lay and his top executives, each one more alarming than the ones that preceded it. By November 2001, Enron's stock price had plummeted from a high of $85 per share to about 30 cents, while its top executives—among them Lay, chief financial officer Andy Fastow and his wife, Lea Fastow, the company's assistant treasurer—were facing criminal charges. And, while all this was going on, the Houston Astros baseball team had to endure the shame of playing their home games at Enron Field, before team officials were able to buy their way out of their naming rights contract for $5 million.

The scandal wiped out the pension accounts of thousands of Enron workers, and ate away at the portfolios of mutual fund managers who had taken a substantial position in the company. It destroyed Arthur Andersen, and hurt dozens of partners in the accounting firm who were nowhere near this mess. Moreover, it led to intense scrutiny of corporate accounting practices, which in turn led to a separate but not totally unrelated scandal that eventually eclipsed the Enron mess in scope and scale. And just how did *that* happen? Well, down at WorldCom, chief executive Bernard Ebbers was forced to resign in disgrace in April 2002, after being hailed as yet another visionary for building his regional telephone service into the nation's second-largest long distance provider. This guy Ebbers, a former milkman and junior high school basketball coach, had somehow built his small Mississippi-based company into a telecommunications giant, and at first blush it was a remarkable story. At one point, Wall Street valued WorldCom at $184 billion, but it soon spiraled into bankruptcy—leaving 18,500 employees across the country without jobs, and erasing untold billions from the ledgers of pension fund managers who had been unlucky enough to take a large position in WorldCom shares. (Unfortunately, the pensions of those loyal WorldCom employees were also wiped out in the collapse.) Ebbers was eventually found guilty on one count of conspiracy, one count of securities fraud, and seven counts of false regulatory filings, all the while claiming innocence of any knowledge of wrongdoing in WorldCom's accounting practices and pointing the finger at his former chief financial officer, Scott Sullivan.

The two bankruptcies left investors reeling, and created a sense of unease and mistrust in the markets. This was understandable. The public trust was tapped out—and rightly so, it seemed. The ripple effect was devastating, and it will most likely remain so for a while, all because of the monumental greed of a few individuals. Here again, I looked on as Lea and Andy Fastow negotiated their plea bargain deals and tried to figure out who would take care of their kids if they both served concurrent sentences, and I couldn't keep myself from wondering what the heck these people were thinking. What kind of world were they making for their children? What kind of values had they inherited from their own parents? How could they possibly have imagined that things would have turned out differently? And at what point, precisely, did they decide to place everything on the line? It makes no sense to me, to put your whole life at stake on the back of a house-of-cards-type scheme that runs so completely counter to an ethical society—one that threatened the security of thousands of innocent employees, and the retirement accounts of millions of trusting investors—and yet there we were, cleaning up after the two biggest messes in the history of corporate America, and having to live with a culture of criminality that seemed to have taken hold in the minds of individual investors who now had good reason to mistrust our business leaders. The only silver lining, I guess, was that there were real consequences to those involved—with the guilty parties made to endure the public shame of "perp walks" and substantial prison sentences and (in some cases) seven-figure fines—even as the consequences reached to millions of innocent victims, through the pension and mutual fund fallout.

THE MUTUAL FUND MESS

A word or two on that fallout, because it hits us where we live, and chases individual investors to the sidelines. More than one hundred of the country's largest mutual funds were examined by the enforcement division of the Securities and Exchange Commission, in an attempt to root out instances of market timing and late trading, and preliminary findings revealed that more than 50 percent of funds had participated in some type of suspicious market timing activities, while 10 percent reported possible late trading violations. (Market timing, although not itself illegal, is the art and practice of moving in and out of mutual funds on a same-day basis, in pursuit of short-term gains; while short-term day-traders can profit handsomely with such moves, returns for other investors who stay in the fund long-term suffer in correlation, so most mutual fund companies discourage the practice and some bar it in their prospectuses. Despite this prohibition, some mutual funds broke their own rules and let the client time their own funds, if the client generated sufficient fees for the mutual fund company.) Even more troubling, more than 30 percent appeared to have disclosed details about specific holdings to select investors, rigging the game against investors who were out of the insider loop.

Mutual funds, which were established in the early 1900s and first regulated under the Investment Company Act of 1940, were intended as a way for the average investor to participate in the markets without the benefit of deep pockets or unlimited institutional resources, have lately been operating under such a cloud of suspicion that many people have taken their investment dollars elsewhere. "It's not one or two bad apples," noted one state prosecutor leading the investigation, reaching for the same anal-ogy I used earlier in predicting a big shake-out in the mutual fund industry. "The whole crate seems to have gone rotten."

The cleanup continues, and frankly I don't think we're doing a good job of it. The Sarbanes-Oxley Act, signed into law in July 2002 and hailed as the most significant change to federal securi-ties laws since the New Deal, has had a deleterious effect on American business. I'll take a lot of heat for this position, I know, and to be fair there have been some real benefits to some of these new provisions, but I see it as a clear case of the government overreacting to what is admittedly a serious, far-reaching prob-lem, one that can't be solved through legislation. Why? Well, for one thing, you can't legislate ethical behavior; you either know the difference between right and wrong, or you don't. And, for another, you can't make innocent people pay a toll for the trans-gressions of their less-than-innocent colleagues.

On the positive side, Sarbanes-Oxley has established a strong set of internal controls that have been embraced by many busi-nesses, and has pushed corporate executives to be more accurate and accountable than ever before. But while the stiffer rules and regulations regarding accounting and auditing procedures sound great in theory, there are many who believe that in actual prac-tice they've been a deterrent to legitimate American businesses. They've put many honest businessmen and women on the de-fensive. They've discouraged risk taking and entrepreneurship. They've tied the hands of our top executives at a time when they might need to search like never before for creative solutions in an increasingly competitive global marketplace. They've been costly, and duplicative, and have left a great many of our business leaders looking over their shoulder when they should be looking ahead.

The upshot? More and more, companies are taking themselves private, in order to avoid the excessive regulations facing public companies. In recent months, companies like Fidelity Federal Bancorp, Niagara Corporation, Corfacts, Anacomp, and KS Bancorp have "gone dark," delisting their stock from the Nasdaq market, in hopes of finding a less restrictive environment in the private sector. Donald R. Neel, chief executive of the Evansville, Indiana, based Fidelity, reported that the delisting would save his small bank about $300,000 per year in additional filing and accounting costs. "Sarbanes-Oxley was designed to provide additional corporate transparency and safeguards for the investing public," he told the *New York Times* in explaining his bank's decision. "Instead, it is prompting companies like ours to become less transparent."

Too, it's becoming harder and harder for top companies to get good people to serve on their boards, or quality executives to apply for top positions—due to the risks and attacks on reporting and financial well-being, and the mounting fear of frivolous litigation. And so we're beginning to see that this so-called corporate reform act, meant to protect the American investor, is in many ways stifling the progress of American business.

THE 60 MINUTES *PHENOMENON*

There's a phenomenon at work in this country that I call the "60 *Minutes* Syndrome," and it's all over this one. There are people in government—well-meaning, honest, and nevertheless misguided people—who have a knee-jerk tendency to see some out-

rage or other on *60 Minutes* on Sunday night, and then to introduce a bill to counter that outrage on Monday morning. Too
often, it seems, the bill is just a Band-Aid to a much deeper problem, or a grandstanding grab at some publicity, and here I think
we've lost the forest for the trees. Think of it: Would a sweeping
set of new laws to help safeguard and watchdog the accounting
practices in publicly held companies have prevented the sweeping irregularities at Enron and WorldCom? Probably not. Would
they prevent such as this from ever happening in the future?
Again, probably not. Why? Well, it's been my experience that
when folks are determined to cheat the system, they'll go out and
cheat the system, no matter how many times you change the
rules or create a new system, so why reinvent the wheel in such
a way that it effectively punishes those honest, hardworking
business leaders who would never have dreamed up any such
wrongdoing in the first place?

Here we are, railing about all the jobs we're losing overseas,
about the competitive edge American businesses seem to have
ceded to their international competitors, and we're putting up all
these impediments to doing business in this country. It's coun-
terproductive. Do you think there are all these impediments facing corporate executives in China? Not at all. In every other free,
industrialized society, entrepreneurs are free to think outside the
box while we have boxed ourselves into a corner with a blizzard
of unnecessary paperwork and regulations. And the most agonizing piece to all this is that the regulators don't seem to know the
first thing about business, operating from a presumption of guilt
on the part of all business leaders and leaving the good guys hamstrung.

I realize, of course, that it's far easier to highlight a solution that isn't working than it is to come up with a better solution, but in this case I don't think we can fix the problem with a new set of rules and regulations. I'm not even sure we need a solution but to return to our traditional ways of doing business and let the enforcement folks at the SEC sort this mess out—and, in the sorting, let the American public take the time to heal and move on. Sure, what these folks did over at Enron and WorldCom and all these other companies was wrong. Dead wrong. It had a cataclysmic impact on corporate America—not just at the companies involved, but across the board. We've all been affected by it. It was terrible. It hurt people. It hurt communities. It slowed job creation. It destroyed families. It wounded our economy. All because a few people wanted to earn another couple million dollars. And, of course, it's destroyed those few people as well. If any one of them had a chance to do it all over again—Ebbers, Sullivan, Lay, the Fastows—they'd do whatever they could to get their reputations back, I'm almost sure of it. How much would they pay to pull the videotapes from the daddy-cams and the mommy-cams that should be monitoring their behavior, and have those tapes destroyed?

Yes, the individuals involved in these scandals have been variously punished. They've been stripped of their reputations, and their positions. They've been substantially fined. They've been sent to prison. There have been consequences all around—and yet no punitive damages or reparations can ever restore stability to the pension funds and mutual funds and individual shareholder accounts that were trashed by their actions, just as no corporate reform act can set things right in a vacuum. If anything, the one encouraging piece to these scandals is that in a society where an apology too often passes for consequences, the guilty parties in our business community have been soundly punished. Justice is being done. It might not be as swift as we'd like it to be in certain cases, but our system of checks and balances appears to be working.

And yet what I find most amazing is that businessmen and -women continue to break the law and push the boundaries of ethical and moral behavior, even as these scandals make headlines. Some people just don't get it, do they? I mean, we've had all these accountants and financial officers carted off to jail, and publicly disgraced, and every week it seems there are bulletins of yet another transgression, in yet another corporate office, and I get to thinking that no amount of negative reinforcement will ever set *everybody* straight. In any case, justice alone cannot set things right, and it comes back yet again to our core values. We don't need the Sarbanes-Oxley Act to tell us the difference between right and wrong. We don't need the government to step in and tell us how to behave, because in the end it comes down to human nature. We don't need to see these shady accountants and CFOs carted off to jail to turn us away from illegal acts that might set us down the same path.

Let me explain what I mean by sharing a recent experience. I lectured at a business class at Ohio State, and during one of my classes the talk turned to ethics. One of my students raised his hand and politely said, "No offense, sir, but why should I believe anything you say when it comes to ethics? You're a former politician."

Everybody had a good chuckle at my expense—myself included.

"Okay," I said. "Point taken, but what are *you* majoring in?"

"Accounting," the young man replied.

At this, I raised my eyebrows and said, "Accounting?"

Everybody had another good chuckle, this time at the student's expense, this being in the wake of all these accounting messes.

The student shrugged it off good-naturedly, but I had stumbled upon an all-important point and I was determined to make it. "Why do you think some of these accounting firms have gone down the tubes?" I asked. "Why do you think we've had all these scandals?"

The student mumbled something about a lack of clarity in some obscure accounting regulation.

"No," I said, shaking my head. "That's the answer I'd expect from a government regulator, but that's not it at all. It has to do with people. Human nature, that's the bottom line."

I went on to paint a scenario that didn't seem all that far-fetched to these jaded young students. "Let's say you're working for an accounting firm," I continued, "and let's say you've been assigned to a client, and after six months or so you realize that somebody was cooking the books. What do you do? You go in to the senior partner and you tell him the numbers aren't adding up and he tells you that if you want to go somewhere in this firm you had better look the other way and keep your mouth shut. That's the proverbial fork in the road, and it's the same fork these Enron guys must have faced, at some turning-point moment before everything got out of hand. It becomes something more than just the mere question of whether or not you can get away with it. For some people, in some situations, it becomes a question of whether or not you can go along in order to get along. It's about doing what you have to do to keep your job, and going against what you know to be right and true just to appease your superiors, and finding a way to live with yourself and your duplicity, and what rules and regulations are we going to come up with to take care of that?"

To be honest, I don't know that my students had the first idea what to make of my diatribe, judging from the open-mouthed looks I got back at the other end, but in the back-and-forth I had stumbled across a compelling distinction—namely, the longer we keep painting *all* business leaders with the same brush as our disgraced business leaders, the longer we'll be digging out from under.

There's a perception out there that our corporations are run by crooks, and that we're just waiting for the next one to get caught, but that's clearly not the case. Anyway, it hasn't been my experience. Most people I know in business work terribly hard at their jobs. They devote themselves fully and wholeheartedly to whatever it is they're making or selling or doing, only to be second-guessed by industry analysts and shareholders at every turn. The overwhelming majority of them are ethical, law-abiding, moral people, with a clear sense of right and wrong, and I find it appalling when people suggest otherwise.

And yet I'll be the first to admit that it's tough to stand and do the right thing when you find yourself in a situation where your boss expects you to stray from the straight and narrow. Let's all recognize that this is a difficult situation and that our lives are shot through with difficult situations. It's tough to tell your boss at the accounting firm that your client is a shady character because you might lose your job. In sports, it's tough to blow the whistle on your steroid-using teammates when your team is winning and selling out all its home games. In politics, it's tough to take a position when your entire party thinks it's a bad idea. It's tough to be a teacher and challenge your own school district to do a better job educating its children. And it's tough to stay in an unhappy marriage for the sake of your kids when all around you friends and colleagues are selfishly setting their marriage vows aside in exchange for a glint of happiness with another partner.

Life is tough. That's a given. Business is tough—another given. But there's no reason to bend to every base impulse, or to conveniently misplace our moral compasses, just to cover our own backsides. That, friends, is not leadership at all—that's *being led*, down the wrong path, for the wrong reasons, and securing a legacy that will haunt you for the rest of your life.

THE ACTIVISION STAND

No, it's never easy to stand alone or buck the system, but it is within reach, and here I'll shine a positive light on a business leader who's made a successful career out of rejecting the base impulses of his industry. Bobby Kotick—or Robert Kotick, to his shareholders and board of directors—is chief executive of Activision, one of the world's leading video game developers and distributors, based in Santa Monica, California. He's also a friend, and from time to time our talk turns to his sense of responsibility, providing video games to a market that is made up almost exclusively of impressionable young people.

Industry-wide, the rap on video games is that they are excessively and gratuitously violent, that they promote the exploitation and denigration of women and minorities, and that they are slowly desensitizing our children to gang violence and school shootings and domestic abuse. I'm afraid the rap is justified. Top-selling titles like *Grand Theft Auto* are brutally graphic, with no redeeming social value, and I can't for the life of me understand how any parent could allow such trash in his household. More than that, I can't understand how the publishers of these games—most of whom are parents themselves—can look themselves in the mirror or find peace enough to sleep at night after marketing that kind of filth to children. (You can just forget about the daddy-cam concept keeping some of these individuals honest, because it's apparent by their conduct that they couldn't possibly care what their children think of them.) There's even a game on the market called *JFK Reloaded* that invites participants to assume the role of Lee Harvey Oswald and re-create the assassination of President Kennedy. At the time of its launch, the company that makes and markets the game offered a cash prize to the player who most closely approximated the trajectories on the three shots fired by Oswald on November 22, 1963, as determined by the Warren Commission. I'm telling you, *despicable* doesn't even begin to describe some of these things.

Bobby Kotick can't understand it either, and he steadfastly refuses to buy into it, so much so that he's committed to only developing games that stay out of the gutter. He's not so high-minded that he avoids shooting games entirely, and I'm sure there's some small measure of blood and gore in his games intended for a more "mature" audience, but he won't make or market these extreme-type titles. He won't sink to that level. His thinking is, there's enough money to be made selling positive images that he doesn't need to traffic in that kind of garbage, and he's willing to leave those ill-gotten gains to his competitors.

Just this past Halloween, I saw an item in the paper about a costume manufacturer who was marketing a line of "pimp" and "ho" outfits to young children, and I thought once again of Bobby Kotick's principled stand. Are we really so desperate to make money that we must peddle Halloween costumes glorifying prostitution to our children? It's the crass limbo of the marketplace—how low can you go to make a buck?—and the refusal to play *that* game is what sets true business leaders like Bobby Kotick apart.

Realize, Activision is a publicly traded company, and its chief executive is made to answer to a board and to investors, and in that kind of environment you can't simply turn away from such a huge center of potential profits. If your competitors are doing it, there's a certain amount of pressure on you to do the same. And yet, Bobby Kotick's company has taken the higher road and performed fantastically well, posting annual net revenues of $1.4 billion, through licensing arrangements with family-friendly companies like Disney. Could Activision make even more money, publishing filth and poisoning the minds of our children and re-creating some of the darkest moments in American history? No doubt about it, but Bobby Kotick has taken a stand, and he's managed to get an entire company to stand behind him.

That's something.

WEIRTON STEEL

It's also something the way some of our top executives lead by shining example, and count themselves beholden to their colleagues, their employees, their shareholders, *and* their creditors— even when they don't have to but for the way they were raised. Consider the rousing case of another friend, John Walker, who used to be the CEO of Weirton Steel, in Weirton, West Virginia. The backstory on Weirton Steel is that it was facing bankruptcy, and there was a provision in John's contract that called for him to receive a one-time payment of approximately $1.3 million if certain conditions were met. When the company filed a voluntary petition to reorganize itself under Chapter 11 bankruptcy proceedings, the Weirton board asked John to stay on, at which point the $1.3 million payment kicked in, but John couldn't justify that kind of windfall. All around, people were losing their pensions, their health benefits, and in some cases their jobs, and he couldn't stomach the thought that he could actually *profit* from their misfortune. Legitimate creditors were being made to line up to collect just a fraction of the monies they were rightfully due, so how could John sleep at night or look himself in the mirror if he walked away with $1.3 million he didn't feel he'd earned?

John Walker was a man of relatively modest means—at least in CEO circles. He didn't have a whole lot growing up, and he didn't have a whole lot more than he needed now that he had arrived at the top of his field, so the $1.3 million was meaningful. It was lifestyle-changing money to a guy like John, which made it all the more difficult to look away from it. Still, he couldn't bring himself to accept it. Everyone he talked to—friends, lawyers, Weirton directors—told him to keep the money, that it was rightfully and contractually his, but it didn't sit right, so he wrote a check for the full amount from his personal account and returned the money to the company.

Realize, too, that John Walker wasn't facing this dilemma alone. There was a Weirton CFO in a similar position, entitled by the same poison-pill-type clause in his contract to receive a payout of about $700,000, and he also wrote a check back to the company—and I mention this second moral act for the way it reinforces the first, and suggests once again that this type of behavior is catching.

"It took my wife and me about fifteen seconds to decide that it was the right thing to do," John Walker says now. "We had no choice but to give that money back. The company was filing for bankruptcy. All I had to do was look in the faces of people who were losing everything, and I knew that money wasn't mine."

WHY CONSCIENCE MATTERS

Happily, John Walker isn't the only business leader with a conscience. In fact, I'm betting that most of our top executives would have acted in the same noble way. I'm particularly heartened when I read about business leaders who encourage employees at every level to take their own stands *outside* the workplace. At Timberland, the outdoor apparel company based in New Hampshire, corporate altruism runs so deep that management allows its workers a full week off each year, with pay, to help out local charities. Even better, the company offers four paid sabbaticals each year, which are put up for grabs to workers looking to sign on for up to six months to work for area nonprofit organizations. And—get this!—the company shuts down its entire operation for one day each year so that its 5,400 workers can participate in various company-sponsored philanthropic projects— at a cost to the company of nearly $2 million in lost sales, project expenses, and wages for workers, who all receive a full day's pay. As a result, the spirit of volunteerism is so much a part of the culture at Timberland that employees wouldn't have it any other way; 95 percent of them do additional volunteer work above and beyond the company-backed efforts, and most report that it was this focus on selflessness that attracted them to Timberland in the first place. For their part, Timberland executives are thrilled at the spillover impact its goodwill has contributed to the for-profit segment of its operation. "People like to feel good about where they work and what they do," explains Timberland CEO Jeffrey Swartz.

Yes they do.

People also like it when their bosses deflect the credit when things go wonderfully right, and take the heat when they go horribly wrong. Accountability is key, and we need look no further than the executive offices at Johnson & Johnson, the pharmaceutical giant, to see a stirring example of same. I'm reaching back into our recent historical archives for this one, but it's such a great story of an American business leader standing tall and doing the right thing in the face of real adversity that it rates a mention here. Remember the Tylenol tampering scare, back in 1982? It began in Chicago, when three people died from cyanide poisoning after taking Tylenol capsules. Soon, cyanide deaths linked to Tylenol were reported all across the country, and Johnson & Johnson chief operating officer James Burke made the swift decision to pull his product from the shelves and suspend all advertising. We look back now and think there was no other move the company could have made, but at the time it was surely an agonizing decision, to recall millions of bottles of Tylenol, at an unfathomable cost to Johnson & Johnson, both in terms of lost revenues (estimated at more than $100 million) and a tarnished corporate reputation. It was the only moral decision facing Burke and his colleagues, but it was agonizing just the same.

The real dilemma, Burke later said, was not whether or not to recall the Tylenol capsules, but how to protect Johnson & Johnson's good name once consumers came to know Tylenol as a Johnson & Johnson product, and so he engaged a public relations firm to survey consumer attitudes toward the company and its products in the wake of these cyanide-tampering incidents. He authorized a straightforward series of television and print advertisements intended to assure loyal customers that Johnson & Johnson was doing everything in its power to ensure that its products were safe and tamper-resistant. And he opened his doors to the media and made sure the press was fully informed on every aspect of the crisis, even when it was discovered that the cyanide had come from a quality assurance factory located next door to the Tylenol manufacturing facility.

In all, Burke's worldwide withdrawal of his product from the marketplace and his absolute candor helped to save his company from disaster, and now, nearly twenty-five years later, the response of the Johnson & Johnson board continues to stand as a model in corporate crisis control.

Too often, it seems, companies in crisis look to backpedal, or obscure the facts to paint their efforts in the best possible light, and it feels a little disingenuous for me to be praising the folks at Johnson & Johnson for merely doing what was right and expected on this one—and yet there's no denying how difficult it must have been, to act with such responsibility and integrity in the face of such a devastating development regarding one of the company's most popular and profitable products. But that's just it. It's not always easy to do the right thing, and still we have no choice but to try.

"Business is a morally serious enterprise, in which it is possible to act either immorally or morally," writes Michael Novak in his book *Business As a Calling: Work and the Examined Life.* "By its own internal logic and inherent moral drive, business requires moral conduct."

Novak has got it right: Business *is* a calling. It's not just about making money, and returning a profit to your investors. It's about building a life—not just for yourself and your own family, but for your colleagues, and employees, and their families as well. It's about making choices, and we all have a choice on this one. We can align ourselves with people like Bobby Kotick, and companies like Johnson & Johnson, and put our shoulder to the wheel and preserve free markets and free enterprise as the jewels they ought to be—or we can side with the Kenneth Lays and Dennis Kozlowskis and take the easy road that can only lead to despair and ruin. It's up to us to decide which team we want to play for, the good guys or the bad guys, both as leaders *and* as consumers. What legacy do you want to leave? It's astounding to me, the number of people who look to cheat the system, even as these cases are made on these falls from grace, and yet I have to believe that over time our ethical business leaders will once again predominate.

Let us put conscience and ethics ahead of profits. Let us demand limited government interference in our free market system, and let us justify that demand by policing ourselves. Let us reinvigorate our capital system and leave it renewed for our children. Let us set temptation aside, and vow not to take any shortcuts to any short-term gains. Let us remind ourselves that our reputations are precious, and that when we disgrace ourselves in business, as in everything else, we also disgrace our families, our friends, and our associates. And let us never forget that in business, as elsewhere, the right thing to do is the only thing to do, and know that until the John Walkers of the world start getting more attention than the Bernie Ebberses I'll be out here sounding the call and shining positive light wherever I can find it.

And I'll be trusting you to do the same.

6

TAKING A STAND
ON RELIGION

"Freedom prospers when religion is vibrant and the rule of law under God is acknowledged."

Ronald Reagan

I read the Bible. I travel with one, in fact, and there's never a time that I don't have a page or a passage bookmarked or flagged for my ready reference. Why? Because the Bible always has something new to teach me, some new way to look at the world, some ancient story that can't help but resonate in interesting ways against the backdrop of our times. Plus, it's the greatest story ever told. Greed and charity, ruin and redemption, misery and hope . . . it's all right there. It's accessible, and at the same time it's beyond knowing, and I can't for the life of me figure how anyone gets along without it.

Do I read it all the time? No, of course not. Do I quote from it constantly, like some Bible-thumping preacher, or use it as a crutch to explain away my transgressions? Once again, no and no. But I keep a copy close at hand and every time I read it I discover something I didn't know before. About myself. About these rich and complex people whose actions have echoed for centuries. About the human condition. About faith.

You see, faith is a curious and wonderful thing, and we live in curious and wonderful times—and this is especially significant when it comes to matters of religion. On the one hand, the pendulum has swung back in recent years to where it's okay for our leaders to openly express their religious views. It's become almost obligatory for our politicians to wear their faith on their sleeves, and I'm not so sure this is a good thing. It's an interesting thing, no question, and it puts faith on the map for a whole lot of people, but I wonder if it encourages some candidates to go to church as a photo opportunity; I wonder if they're just going through the motions and setting the wrong kind of example for those of us who consider these things deeply.

On the other hand, the rest of us are still playing our faith close to the vest. I've got a good friend named Dick Vogt who's a member of my Bible study group, and he's always telling us he's not about to talk about his religion anywhere, because it's not politically correct and because people start to look at him like he's some sort of a nut case if he even brings up the subject. He says there is a disdain in many social circles with regard to religion, and I'm afraid he's right, and he avoids the topic because he doesn't want to be an outcast, and yet that's what's so curious and wonderful about the state of religion in today's society: Politicians are encouraged to be open with regard to their faith— as are actors and athletes and other celebrity-types, to a certain extent—while the rest of us are encouraged to keep our mouths shut, and the reason we're encouraged to keep our mouths shut is because a lot of people have the opinion that religion is based on condemnation and judgment. To many, it's all about what you might have done wrong, and how you might have failed, and how you might repent. There's a whole lot of sticking of noses into other people's business, and yet there's no sense of grace, or openness, or inclusion, so of course people aren't talking about it at cocktail parties.

WHY RELIGION MATTERS

I wonder at this dichotomy, and I have to think it has to do with our inability to understand the challenges of today and translate them to the challenges of yesterday. The problems and the answers are the same. The players might be different. The details might be different. But in big-picture terms, it's all the same. There are no new dilemmas.

I want to begin this discussion on a personal note, because I believe it's appropriate here. After all, faith is a very personal matter, and I find myself longing for a time when we can *all* talk about it, honestly and openly. In my own life it flows from my parents. Let me just reiterate a couple of points before making some new ones: I grew up in and around the church. I was an altar boy. For a long time I thought I'd become a priest, and yet as I made my way in the world I seemed to inch away from the foundation my parents had laid for me. Mind you, I continued to believe in God—although for a time in there I confess I came to regard Him as a kind of spiritual Santa, someone to give me the presents I was seeking. I continued to go to church, although not as frequently as I might have. I even continued to pray, although here, too, the depth and resonance of my prayers were not what they had been or what they would become. Most important, I continued to live my life in ways that were consistent with the values I learned from my parents and that had been reinforced for me over the years. But there was very definitely a drift, a change in emphasis; it wasn't all-important the way it had once been. It wasn't a defining aspect of character, the way I once longed for it to be. I became set in my ways, as often happens, and I looked up one day and realized I hadn't made the kind of room in those ways for religion. I wasn't as plugged in as I wanted to be and I didn't really care to get back to it.

Lord knows, I couldn't blame this one on anyone but myself. My parents brought me to the doors of our church, and they held those doors open for me throughout my growing up, but like many young people I began to walk away at some point. It no longer seemed relevant. The rest of my life got in the way. That's no excuse, but that's just how it was.

Now, here's where it gets personal . . .

My parents, John and Anne Kasich, were children of immigrants. My father's family came from Czechoslovakia; my mother's family came from Yugoslavia. They met when they were both working for the Veterans Administration following World War Two. My dad delivered mail for twenty-nine years; our house was on his route. My mom eventually worked at the post office in Pittsburgh, once we kids were out from underfoot. Here again, I mentioned some of these things earlier, when I wrote about my childhood, but I reiterate them here for a reason. My parents were honest, hardworking, God-fearing people. They didn't drink or smoke or spend money to excess. My mother would sooner walk a mile than spend a quarter to ride the city bus, and my father was equally thrifty. They were in their late sixties, in perfect health, looking ahead to a long, fulfilling retirement, when a drunk driver crashed into their car as they were leaving a Burger King one cool summer night in August 1987. The devastating paradox here is that they almost never went out to eat, but they went to Burger King because they liked the coffee, which was also a bargain.

I got a call just before midnight from a doctor telling me my father had been killed and that my mother was in critical condition. It knocked the wind right out of me and sent me reeling. I rode straight through the night with the woman I was seeing at the time (she did all the driving), and as we pulled into Pittsburgh we got behind a tar truck and the next thing we knew our windshield was covered in black tar. It was just about dawn, the sun inching over the horizon, and it didn't occur to me at the time but I wonder now if that wasn't some kind of sign. My world had gone black, and I couldn't see my way clear to what might come next—and here, now, it had gone black in a very literal sense as well. Nothing like this had ever happened to me before, and nothing like this has ever happened since. Goodness, I'd never even heard of anybody getting stuck behind a tar truck and getting sprayed in just this way, but there it was. We actually had to pull over and use shampoo to cut through the tar, just to be able to see again, and every now and then I get to thinking about that long, frantic night and I get this weird image of me standing by the side of the road, just outside Pittsburgh, rubbing shampoo into this film of black tar on the windshield of the car in the bright orange of dawn.

I don't really remember any other particulars of the trip, but we somehow made it. My mother was still alive when I got to the hospital, but I never got to talk to her, or tell her I loved her. She died later that morning, and when she did I sat for a while with a kind man named Stu Boehmig, the assistant pastor at my parents' Episcopal church. Stu tried to comfort me, but I was beyond comforting. He tried to tell me he knew just how I felt, but I couldn't hear it. In fact, I railed against it.

"How can you know how I feel?" I said heatedly. "No one can possibly know how I feel."

I should never have spoken to Stu in such a harsh way, but I wasn't myself, and to Stu's great credit he understood. He let my anger slide. He said, "John, you're right. No one can possibly know how you feel. But I do know that your mother would rather be with her Lord than anyplace else. She wouldn't come back if she had the chance."

Stu Boehmig's good counsel was the first piece of comfort I could find in those dark, surreal hours just after the accident, and he wasn't done yet. A couple days later, he went on to offer words of hope and a challenge I took very much to heart.

"John," he said, "you've got to decide right now if you want to build a relationship with God. You have a window of opportunity now, you're open to it, but in time that window will close. This pain will ease and you'll go back to the rest of your life."

TURNING BACK TO GOD

Right there, in just that moment, I knew Stu was right. I knew I had moved away from God in my life, and that I had no place else to turn to get through the days ahead. I knew intuitively that this was my one chance to reconnect with the faith of my growing up, in a lifelong and sustaining way. And from that moment forward, I changed. Really and fully and truly. They say people can't change, but I became the argument against that truism, and my parents' deaths started a long, ten-year journey not just to return to religion but to investigate the deep reality of it—to *own* it, once more. I was determined to spend the time questioning everything formal religion taught, and at the same time figure out if I could build a real relationship with God, if He could stand for me as a strength, a friend, a father, a direction. The *real* relationship was key. I wanted real, not learned. Not rote. Not symbols. Not dogma. Reality, that's what I was after. Did Jesus really live? Why do we think he rose from the dead? Did he really get crucified? And what did all of this mean to me and my family and friends as we turned headlong into the twenty-first century? These became the burning questions of my days, and I'd find myself in Bible study groups back in Washington asking all kinds of off-the-wall questions. There are people out there who probably still think of me as a complete crackpot, because of the way I was so desperately searching in those days, but I was determined to get to the heart of what faith really meant.

I set out these circumstances to illustrate how keenly important it was for me to let religion back into my life. Now, with perspective and healing, I don't know how people survive that kind of pain without faith. My parents' deaths began a transformation for me, a journey to discover God and to rediscover myself that continues to this day, as it will continue for all my days. Religion became a source of strength and solace and balance.

With faith, I learned, comes peace. I also learned that it's not an easy road that takes us to God, but with exercise, discipline, and prayer, I make strides. Every day, I make strides. Anyway, I mean to.

Okay, so that's me. That's where I'm at with this thing, and how committed I am to it, and how it sits front and center in regard to everything I do. Yes, I know full well that not everyone is cut the same way. Yes, I know that there's room in this whole wide world for people of all different faiths, and all different religions, and all different forms and manner of worship. Yes, I might choose one path, but there are other paths. Yes, I know that you can roll a bowling ball in the great cathedrals of Europe on any given Sunday and not hit a soul, that's how disconnected and disaffected the folks over there have come to be about religion. And yes, I know that even in the United States, a nation built on the back of Judeo-Christian ideals, you might need to look long and hard before finding a like-minded individual when it comes to matters of faith. Like I said, we're all cut a little differently, and that will just have to be okay, but what troubles me is how far removed some of us have become from our own foundations. I don't care what you believe, as long as you believe in something—something bigger than yourself and larger than life and greater than any good we can manage on our own. We can't compare ourselves to each other on this one, only to the kind of people we meant to be when we were younger, the kind of people our parents meant us to be, the kind of people we hope to become, still.

"WHAT A GREAT GIG!"

I'll illustrate my concern with a story. I was at the FOX News studios in New York one afternoon about a year or so after I left

Congress, working with a group of mostly young producers. They were all well-educated and well-meaning media types, some fresh out of college and working their first or second jobs in television. I was in my new element, as a television commentator, and I loved working with these people. I tended to think of them as the gatekeepers of the future, because I knew that in ten or twenty years they'd be the ones running our network and cable news programs, deciding what gets on the air, how it gets reported, and where to place the emphasis on the news of the day. In all, a bright group of young people, with a strong respect for the power of television and the responsibility that came along with that power.

One of the lead news stories on this particular day was the shooting down of a small plane that had been carrying a family of missionaries in Peru. The mother and daughter had been killed in the crash, while the father and son had miraculously survived, and as I sat with these young producers discussing the segment for that night's show I overheard the strangest, most unsettling comment from one of my young colleagues.

"What a great life these missionaries have," noted one of the female producers in the room with us at the time. "They get to travel the world and go to all these great places!"

Understand, there was no irony in this young woman's voice, no cool detachment and all kidding aside. She'd processed the missionary work of these good people as if they'd signed on for some exotic adventure tour, never once considering that it was a calling. I was absolutely stunned, not least because this was in every other respect a savvy, insightful person. I was so stunned, in fact, that at first I could not think of a single thing to say, and those who know me will allow that such as this doesn't happen all that often. Of course, I did say something eventually, but it didn't do any good. It just made me look like some crazy zealot. And still this poor young woman kept going on and on about what a great travel experience these missionaries were having—*what a great gig!*—and how they were getting to see all these out-of-the-way places for free, and I thought, She just doesn't get it. And then of course I realized it wasn't just her. More and more, our young people are so far removed from the kind of calling that would compel an individual to take up missionary work that they can't possibly understand it. It's off the map of their experience, so they try to reduce it to what they know, and I started to think her tossed-off comment—however innocent, however igno-rant—was emblematic of the deep chasm we face when it comes to matters of faith.

SHARING THE GIFT

I was reminded of a conversation I'd had with Father Tim Scully of Notre Dame, early on in the abuse scandal that continues to rock the Catholic Church. I was curious to know the church's latest thoughts on celibacy in light of these developments, so I sought him out at a time when a lot of folks in the country were having a hard time reconciling all these allegations of sexual abuse at the hands of priests around the world. I wondered if he thought priests should be allowed to marry.

"John," he said, "what people have a hard time conceiving is that I have dedicated my life to the love of God. I am married with my love and commitment to the service of God. And it's a gift to me. It's not a chore or a sacrifice. It's a gift."

I thought it was a fantastic answer to what Father Scully probably heard as a stupid question—a gift!—but even as I marveled at the devoutness of it I couldn't shake thinking it was probably a tough concept for a lot of folks to truly understand. I mean, it's the twenty-first century, and people just don't get it. They get what it means to believe in God, and to pray, but they start to lose the signal when the talk turns to worship and devotion. Even some of our educated, media-savvy young people don't get it, as evidenced by that poor FOX News producer, and yet we need to somehow ensure that enough people truly understand it in order to sustain it.

That's the real challenge facing today's religious leaders—how to remain rooted and relevant to the lives of our young people while at the same time holding fast to tradition—and I'm not always certain that they're up to it. I'd felt for the longest time that the Catholic Church had been losing its moorings, and I think Pope John Paul II did a glorious job returning to Catholics a sense that the church was not about the culture of today so much as it was committed to a set of principles that were biblically founded. It's classic, and timeless, and unshakable. The enormous outpouring of love and devotion upon his death on April 2, 2005, was vibrant testimony of his achievement in this all-important area, and this was especially so among our young people. I had the same feeling when he appeared before a large audience that I had when I was with Ronald Reagan on a stage at Ohio State University, in front of ten thousand screaming students. If I hadn't known it was Reagan, I'd have thought it was Bono, and Pope John Paul II evoked the same kind of adulation. And, indeed, the numbers bore this out, as teens and young adults returned to the church in record numbers during his papacy—a great many of them devoting their lives to it.

Young people love to believe in things, wouldn't you agree? They love it when people and institutions are exact and firm and principled. They love it when you stand for something. They're drawn to stability, and strength, and they were drawn to this pope, without question. From the outset, they were drawn to him, a little known Polish cardinal, and he built on that as he went along. Really, his leadership qualities were astonishing. The humility he demonstrated whenever he got off a plane and kissed the tarmac. The compassion he showed when he visited the prison cell of Mehmet Ali Agca, the Turkish terrorist who tried to assassinate him in 1981, and forgave him his sins. The warm embrace he extended to leaders and followers of different faiths, and to Jews in particular. And, above all, and as a kind of exclamation point, the way he shouldered his suffering at the very end. In a world where our heroes are almost always discredited, Pope John Paul II was able to live a life without missteps, and to go out in a way that was graceful and dignified and inspiring. I don't care if you're Catholic or Muslim or atheist, it was impossible not to be moved by this man—and in the long sigh left by his passing, and the long lines of mourners that formed outside St. Peter's Basilica to pay their respects, we could find the points of connection we'll need to stand on firm religious ground once more.

His death called to mind one of the most indelible images of my growing up—my mother, crying. She was no longer alive to cry for this pope, but she cried for Pope John XXIII. It was 1963, and it was one of the few times I can recall seeing her moved to tears, which of course meant the sight moved me to same. As long as I'm on it, I'll close out this reflection by mentioning one other time I saw my mother cry, upon the death of Pittsburgh Pirates legend Roberto Clemente, the Puerto Rican–born baseball great who was an icon in our part of the world, and one of my true boyhood heroes. Clemente died on a relief mission to Nicaragua in 1972, and news of his death hit our household hard—and I was surprised to see my mother so shaken by it.

She would have been shaken by the passing of Pope John Paul II as well, because of the light he managed to bring to the church and to the world around. See, Pope John Paul II may have been socially progressive, but he was a theological conservative, and in his hands the two were not mutually exclusive. He was able to create moorings through his love of mankind, and build bridges from who we are today to how we've been for centuries. Through his love of *all* individuals, he delivered the powerful message that if you truly love another person, then you will listen to that other person, even if you don't agree with him. He threaded the needle and made the church relevant to a swelling mass of people who had drifted, while at the same time extolling the ideals upon which it was built. And it was critical, because as Jesus Christ once said in another context, if you're not really salt then you're not getting anybody's attention. In other words, if the salt goes bad, then there's no kick to it, no purpose, and if our religious leaders can't figure this out we've all lost.

FALLS FROM GRACE

Sad to say, some of our most visible leaders give religion a bad name. Disgraced priests, rabbis, ministers . . . they preach one thing and do another and their duplicity is seized upon by skeptics or opponents of religion to discredit the faith. The troubling piece here is that the misdeeds of these few individuals have also damaged the reputations of others by association, and I'm reminded of that old philosophical puzzle: Just because I'm in a garage and say I'm a car doesn't make it so. Just because these people claim to be holy and pious doesn't make them holy and pious, but they've laid claim to some pretty significant territory here and stained it by their actions, again by association.

I also worry that when the central message of religion is fear and punishment, the true meaning of faith, hope, and grace is lost. I've stated earlier that the rules are a given in religion, but when they dominate center stage, and emphasize our failures, it ceases to have any appeal as a way of life. Those preachers and evangelists who kick up dust and yell and scream and condemn, who seek to shame us into following the path *they've* chosen for us, are off target. Grace, forgiveness, and an opportunity to improve your life is the essence of *my* Christian faith.

Philip Yancey, the best-selling writer of books like *What's So Amazing About Grace?* and a former editor-at-large at *Christian Today* magazine, relates a compelling story that speaks to just this point. He tells of a woman whose daughter has strayed and become a prostitute; the mother reaches out everywhere she can for help until someone finally suggests she go to church. "That's the last place I'll ever go," she says, and in the grace note to the tale there is an immutable truth that gets to just how disconnected some people feel when it comes to religion.

In my opinion, men of faith must be careful not to let politics creep into the pulpit, because you disenfranchise people who might disagree with you. It's happened to me a number of times, in a number of churches, when I've caught myself disagreeing with the political message and wondering about the credibility of the spiritual message. Absolutely, I understand the frustration people of faith have when the culture seems to move against them, but a preacher's macro job is to change the hearts of the people in power and let the rest take care of itself. More than ever before, today's preachers must be careful not to change platforms, and not to confuse their calling or the work of God with secular lawmaking.

Even the Reverend Billy Graham, another one of my personal heroes, was criticized early on in his ministry for his close ties to U.S. presidents and other elected officials. "I did take sides in some things, even in politics to an extent," he admitted to *USA Today* on the eve of his 417th crusade in May 2005. "I didn't mean to, but I did. But I don't do that anymore. If I took sides in all these divisive areas, I would cut off a great part of the people that I really want to reach. So I've felt that the Lord would have me just present the Gospel."

My own minister is sometimes guilty of this—albeit on a much smaller scale. He's a guy I admire and respect, but when he talks politics he starts to lose me, and if he loses me with his politics he's liable to lose me in other ways as well. Let's face it, if he sees the world in one way politically, then how do I know that the way he interprets Scripture isn't colored in some of those same ways? How do I know that he's not just trying to bend the text to win some political argument? He happens to be a liberal, but that's besides the point. I don't go to church to hear a political sermon; I go to be moved, and lifted, and inspired; I go to reflect on the stuff of my life, considered against all these illuminating stories in the Old and New Testaments.

I happen to like my preacher a whole lot, and I consider him a friend, so I'm willing to forgive him on this one, but most folks aren't going to cut their own preachers such slack. Most folks hear the politicking and tune out, and I can't really blame them. I'll never forget sitting one Sunday morning in an Episcopal church, and for no good reason the minister started reading a letter from the bishops discussing why we shouldn't put missiles in Europe. I stood straight up and left. I thought, What do these bishops know about missiles in Europe? Fact is, it was those very missiles in Europe that bolstered the historic negotiations that ultimately led to the tearing down of the Berlin Wall, but I didn't walk out because the politics was all wrong. I walked out because, right or wrong, it had no place in the church.

I even dragged my daughter Reese into taking another such stand—this time at my own church. It was the fall of 2001, just a few weeks after September 11, and she was about two years old. Some woman minister stood up and declared that the only thing the United States had ever exported to the world was *Baywatch*, implying that in some way Americans deserved to be attacked, and I wasn't about to sit and listen to that kind of nonsense, so I collected Reese in my arms and stormed out. It was the only time I've ever walked out of my own church, and I don't expect to be walking out again any time soon, but this was just too much.

I called my wife on the cell phone on my way out to the car and said, "Honey, Reese was involved in her first protest today." I made a joke out of it, but it was no joke. I even ended up calling the pastor and lighting into him for allowing such a discussion to take place on his watch—and by the time I was through with him he couldn't help but agree with me.

I know how I feel when a liberal minister starts preaching to me, so I can just imagine how liberals must feel when they hear conservative preachers lining up politically. They're spilling their authority over into areas where they have been granted no such authority, and it can't help but set people off. Let's never forget that our preachers hold a tremendous position of power, conferred upon them because of a presumed commitment to serve God. They do not have the right to spill that authority over into a sphere in which they have not been conferred any authority. It drives an unnecessary wedge into what is already a tenuous relationship for many people—namely, their relationship to God.

Don't get me wrong, I believe I have the right to an opinion on the world around me, and sometimes that opinion extends to issues of faith, but losing sight of the power of grace and forgiveness is deadly. The views of Pope John Paul II were strongly conservative, but his love of people and humanity allowed him to express himself firmly and yet effectively. He was heard, when so many others who seemed to condemn were not.

That said, the concept of worship remains a struggle, particularly for our young people. *Believing* comes easily to many of us, but to my thinking religion is more than mere belief; *worshipping* puts it at a whole other level. Christian or Jew, Buddhist or Muslim, it's all the same. It's a tough sell. It's hard enough to get down on your hands and knees and give thanks to a higher power. It was difficult for me, until I opened my arms to it, so I know what it's like to be on the jaded or disillusioned end of this discussion.

THE GREATEST STORIES EVER TOLD

For me, the stories of the Bible are the lure. I'd read them first as a kid, and then again as a young adult, but for some reason the stories didn't speak to me at first. They were just stories. But each time I went back to them, and looked at them from whatever new perspective I had taken in my own life, I took away something new. These days, I participate in a Bible study group with some friends of mine in and around Columbus, including Dick Vogt, whom I mentioned earlier. We've been meeting every other week for about fifteen years, just seven or eight of us, and not a Goody Two-shoes in the bunch. And we've become great friends. We read the Bible, but it's a jumping-off point to so much more. We talk about our lives. We talk about our families. We talk about our hopes and our fears. We talk about integrity. We talk about doing the right thing. Sometimes, I sit among this group and think, This is me, building and sustaining my relationship with God. This is what religion ought to be about. It's not some gooey, intangible, unknowable thing. It's life. And, it's how to navigate that life successfully, and morally, and responsibly. No one in our group has all the answers, and even as a group, taken together, we don't have all the answers. But we do our best. We learn from one another. As important, we learn from our mistakes. We consider them. And we strive to be the better for having made them.

Together, we wonder at the rootlessness of many American families, at the disappearing guideposts in a society that seems to move further and further away from organized religion. Church attendance is at an all-time low in too many of our communities, which means our shared moral compass is harder to find than ever before. Passing on values to the next generation? You can pretty much forget about it without the rudder of faith to help chart the way—and yet we remain ever hopeful that goodness and justice and light will prevail.

One of the great leaps we made in our thinking was not to

look on the Bible as a set of rules and restrictions. That's what puts people off to religion. They see it as restrictive, but we've chosen to see it as a roadmap for success, to keep us from spinning out of orbit. We don't really like all these rules, but we know they're good for us, and that they're meant to keep us from drowning in quicksand or going over the edge of a cliff. They're not meant to deny us this or that good time, or to keep us from doing something that might be really cool. They're the positive boundaries to a life purposefully lived. In this way, we can look on the Bible itself as a kind of roadmap, filled with warning signs but also with signs that encourage certain types of positive behavior. We can't possibly get it right each and every time—we are, after all, human—but the key is in the effort. The key is in recognizing and celebrating what we have, and what we've built, and what we've learned. The ability to get out of bed in the morning, and to breathe and to see and to speak and to listen . . . these are gifts from God, and I'd better be recognizing them as such or I'll lose sight of what really matters. I tell my wife all the time, when I try to explain where I'm at with my faith and my relationship to God, that I'm not off in search of the meaning of life so much as I've undertaken a lifelong effort to understand the mystery and magnificence of God.

Back to the Bible. Most of us know the story of Ruth. She was a devout young woman whose husband died, leaving her to live in her husband's home with her mother-in-law, Naomi, along with another daughter-in-law named Orpon. Naomi's husband and two sons had all died, and she had no one in the world but these two devoted daughters-in-law, whom she urged to go back to their own mothers. "May the Lord grant each of you will find rest in the home of another husband," she generously said to her two daughters-in-law, whereupon Orpon bade her mother-in-law goodbye as Ruth clung to her.

"Don't urge me to leave you or to turn back from you," Ruth said. "Where you go, I will go. And where you stay, I will stay. Your people will be my people, and your God my God. Where you die, I will die, and there I will be buried. May the Lord deal with me be it ever so severely if anything but death separates you and me."

Now, if the story ended right there, it would pack a powerful lesson about devotion and commitment and honor, but it continued. Ruth stayed on in her mother-in-law's home, and she ended up meeting and marrying a wealthy man named Boaz, and she bore him a son, Obed, who became the father of Jesse, in the line of Jesus. She rose to a place of honor and stature in her mother-in-law's village because she didn't take the easy way out—and that to me is more powerful still. She didn't do these things because she sought honor and stature, but because for her they were the right things to do. It's hard to fault the other daughter-in-law, Orpon, for returning to her people, but in Ruth's mind her place was beside her mother-in-law, and she took it gladly, and without bitterness, and she was rewarded for it.

When Jesus asks, "Let he who is without sin cast the first stone," we read between the lines and know that we probably shouldn't pay so much attention to the speck in our neighbor's eye when we've got a log stuck in our own. We ought to get our own houses in order before we look upon our neighbors'.

We can sit in our study group and consider the implications of these passages for hours, but they all come down to honor and faith and integrity and all those good things, wouldn't you agree? They don't beat you over the head and tell you what you have to do in this type of situation, or even what you ought to do, just what you might do. They're guideposts, that's all, but they're enormously compelling and instructive guideposts. They frame the choices that others have made throughout recorded human history, and ask us to consider the consequences of those choices against some of our more modern dilemmas.

I'm troubled by the shift in our cultural signposts, I truly am. I'm troubled by a pop culture phenomenon like Paris Hilton, and the violent, misogynist content of certain rap music videos. I'm troubled because we seem to have lost our moral compass, and because there seems to have been a precipitous decline in our shared values, even as the Old and New Testaments shine as lighthouses in a sea of shifting standards and situational ethics.

Most folks know where they stand when it comes to religion, and spirituality, and matters of good and evil. Most of this stuff is written on our hearts, and I guess it's instinctive. But we must renew the real meaning of religion, and stand up for it once more. In a world confused about its purpose. In a world where the magic of technology gives us a sense that we are in charge. In a world of incredible materialism where "success" too often trumps humility and ethics. Realize, the end is not upon us just yet. It's a difficult message, I know, but the further and further we move from the sanctity and purity of religion, the harder it will be to stand together for a common purpose. We can come at it from different angles, but what counts is that we come at it at all. If you don't want to pray to my God, or read my Bible, that's okay. I might feel sorry for you, but you're not my enemy. We can still stand together on this one. We can still learn from each other. There's room enough for our separate journeys, as long as we recognize that we're seeking many of the same things, that our seeking is built on many of the same ideals, and that all good things flow from the reality of worshipping a higher power.

I've learned over the years that leadership is doing, not saying, and this applies to matters of religion as well. People of faith should talk less and do more. People of faith who are kind, ethical, optimistic, and humble tend to stand out in a crowd, and we need for them to stand tall—now, more than ever before. Americans are in search of meaning. Money, fame, power, and all other earthly honors fall short of satisfying that haunting search for meaning, and I have to think that the reason so many people flocked to see *The Passion of the Christ* in movie theaters is that we're hungry for something more. Absolutely, we're searching for the values and the structure and the meaning and the purpose we left behind in our childhoods. We might be satisfied or quietly content with our lives, and yet many of us are restless and recognize that there's a spiritual hole we're looking to fill in what ways we can. That's what that movie tapped into, I think, and what we need to take away from it is the certainty that people of faith need to demonstrate these time-tested principles in their daily walk. Don't just preach goodness, but do good. Don't just talk about faith, but live it. Take back America not by laws but by example. Offer conscience to a society that too often appears to careen wildly out of control. Americans today are hungry for this type of leadership, and it falls to people of faith to provide it, because I'm afraid it just isn't going to come from anyplace else.

It's easy to claim that we live in a world of darkness, with all of the negative images that flash across the nightly news screen, that we're all stuck behind the same tar truck on a Pittsburgh highway, struggling to look through the windshield. But there's a lot of lightness out there. And we seem to want to walk in that light, as much as possible.

FAITH IN CRISIS

Remember that gripping story, back in the spring of 2005, when an Atlanta woman was held hostage in her own apartment by the suspect in a series of courthouse slayings? The hostage's name was Ashley Smith; the alleged courthouse shooter was Brian Nichols, who was accused of killing four people and wounding a fifth; and the two of them became entwined in a deeply personal standoff that left the hostage counseling the hostage-taker. On God. On family. On purpose. And, perhaps most compellingly, on Nichols's faith-based surrender.

Ashley Smith was no stranger to violence. Her husband had been stabbed to death four years earlier, and she was left to single-parent the couple's five-year-old daughter, Paige, who was off at a church function when her mother was abducted. Smith took the time during which she was held captive to tell Nichols about her daughter, about their connection to their church, about the repairs she had managed to make to her broken heart and her broken family with the strength of her beliefs. She talked to Nichols about the salvation that lay in wait for him if only he could see his way into police custody without any more killings. Ultimately, she talked Nichols down to where he surrendered peacefully to law enforcement officials summoned to the scene by Smith's 911 call.

"I believe God brought him to my door," Smith told reporters, shortly after the manhunt for Nichols had reached its peaceful conclusion.

Indeed, there was such a spiritual connection between captor and captive that upon leaving Smith's home in police custody a cuffed Nichols turned back to his former hostage and said, "Will you tell Paige hello for me?"

Once she was in the glare of the public spotlight, Smith revealed that she was a recovering methamphetamine addict at the time of her abduction, and that she even offered some of her stash to Nichols when her captor began looking about her house for alcohol or marijuana, but in my mind this does nothing to diminish her strength of character under extremely challenging circumstances. In fact, she later told me on my FOX News show that the moment she declined to take the drugs with Nichols was the moment she began to beat her addiction.

I need look no further than Ashley Smith to know that faith and hope reside in us all. I need look no further than that group of schoolchildren in Kentucky, whose parents were all on welfare, raiding their little piggy banks to collect money for the relief effort following that killing tsunami in Southeast Asia to know that there is goodness and light in this world. Or to doctors who continue to make house calls, or teachers who stand up for their students, or carpenters and tradesmen who donate their time to build low-income housing.

And on and on.

Consider, once again, the timeless and powerful message of St. Augustine, who wrote in his *Confessions* all the way back in the fifth century that each of us is blessed in our own unique way. I mentioned this book earlier, in my introductory remarks, and I mention it again here because it's one of my favorites. It has a whole lot to teach us. We all have our gifts, Augustine maintains, and it falls to us to unwrap them and share them with the rest of the world, and once we do there will be goodness all around. We find those gifts in this realm by standing up and being counted. Trust in something bigger than yourself and we shall all be rewarded. Look up into the night sky and know that as the stars shine bright so, too, shall you. Become a part of the constellation. Have faith.

7

TAKING A STAND ON EDUCATION

"The principal goal of education in the schools should be creating men and women who are capable of doing new things, not simply repeating what other generations have done; men and women who are creative, inventive and discoverers, who can be critical and verify, and not accept, everything they are offered."

Jean Piaget

Here's a distressing thought: The United States consistently ranks at or near the bottom among developed nations in every quantifiable category that measures achievement and preparedness in school age children. No less an authority than Bill Gates, one of the smartest guys going when it comes to our ability to compete in a technological world, says our primary and secondary school system simply doesn't work. He's right, it doesn't, and I'm not alone in suggesting that it's not about to work anytime soon.

Sadly, we're just whistling past the graveyard when it comes to primary and secondary school education in this country, and one of these days we'll look up and see that everyone else has passed us by. We simply don't have the rigor, the control in the class-room, the innovation, or the personnel to keep pace, and for too long we've pit school administrators, teachers, and other establishment types against the parents in a battle that neither side can hope to win. Our public school leaders are reluctant to take any action or bring about substantive change because they're afraid they're going to get sued, or they fear the loss of market share, or they worry they'll innovate themselves straight out of their own jobs. More often than not, it's just too darn easy to let the status quo prevail. And our kids are flat-out losing. We're cheating them out of their future, is what it comes down to, and denying them the kind of level playing field to which they ought to be entitled, and the long-term ramifications for our nation's economic future are indeed troubling.

Consider: The world is changing at the speed of thought. The rise to prominence of population giants like China and India, coupled with the easy access to cheap labor worldwide, threatens America's basic industries. Don't get me wrong, there is a rich history of American manufacturing that remains a kind of lifeblood in many of our communities, and America will always make things, but trends point against real sustainable growth in this area. That's a shame, because on a personal level I have a deep attachment to making things (my uncles worked in the steel mills!), and yet it's clear even to me that our strength as a nation lies in intellectual property, our ability to create breakthrough technologies in communication, medicine, manufacturing processes and disruptive technologies that transform human behavior—like cell phones, and jet airplanes, and cure-all vaccines.

WHY EDUCATION MATTERS

I'm not the only one worrying that our public schools have been leaving our kids in the dust. Our tired public school system is logjammed, broken-down, paralyzed . . . and it's been unable to reform itself. That's because it's beyond fixing, I'm afraid. I'm not just talking about schools in our inner cities; the problem runs to our small towns as well, and all across the country, and I hate to paint every public school district with the same brush of gloom and doom but the problem is too widespread to be considered on any kind of individual basis. It's endemic, and systemic, and I sometimes worry we'll never dig ourselves out from all these years of neglect and malaise. To be sure, there are glowing exceptions to my sweeping generalities—and I'll shine a light on a couple in just a bit—but it's on an individual basis that we get ourselves into trouble. It's elementary. People tend to look at their local schools the way they look at their congressmen; they might not like what's going on in Congress, but they support their local congressman. They might not think the education system is working, but they like their kid's teacher, or they think her heart is in the right place or that she's doing the best she can. And that might actually be the case, because teachers tend to be a dedicated, passionate lot. Understand, I've got nothing against our teachers. By and large, they're the under-the-radar heroes in the lives of our children, and it's only through their extra efforts that we're even able to hold our heads above water on this one. But their hands are tied by an antiquated system that has run its course, and we are duty-bound to give them the resources they need in order to do their job to the best of their considerable abilities, and the room to reform a system that is in desperate need of an overhaul.

In contrast, higher education has in place a dynamic model of competing for the right to educate our children, and it's the envy of the world. Somehow, at the undergraduate and graduate school levels, we've managed to get it right—and the reason we get it right, I think, is because schools are forced to compete with one another. That's the real bottom line. Public institutions and private, it's much the same, and our system of higher education will continue to thrive as long as competition for students and their almighty tuition dollars remains strong.

In the interest of full disclosure, I'll state once again (for the record, this time) that I teach at Ohio State University, my alma mater, which may or may not explain why I look favorably on academia these days. In fact, I used to hold a dim view of higher education as well, until I was in its middle and saw it as a boundless opportunity to think, discuss, and innovate. It's certainly given me a new perspective on it, but I don't think I've taken a biased view. Rather, it's as a direct result of this front-row seat to the doings on one of the largest public university campuses in the country that I've come to realize what a tremendous national resource we have in our state university systems. American college campuses continue to attract a great many international students, primarily because our system encourages diversity, innovation, and independent thinking in a way not found on campuses abroad, where professors are often bound by traditions and academic models that no longer seem relevant. And more to the point, there are so many choices in American higher education that the competition for our best and brightest students has forced administrators to keep ahead of the curve and out on the cutting edge.

The rap on higher education in some circles is that our campuses lean a little bit to the left—and there's some truth to that, even though I don't see a whole lot of harm. Yes, college professors tend to be a bit more liberal than conservative—maybe not in our schools of engineering, but certainly in the social sciences—but I don't think that this is anything to get all that worked up about. By the time we send them off to college, our kids should be well equipped to make informed decisions and to think for themselves; the political views of the professor standing at the lectern shouldn't be an issue, and yet there have been bills introduced in various state legislatures seeking to regulate the political content of some of these classes. I hear this and think, Get over it, people. There are so many things to worry about in this life, and I'm afraid this is just not one of them, and there should be no legislating academic freedom, not least because college kids don't need to be spoon-fed their educations in some watered-down way; teaching is more than just spouting off, and we need to give these professors room to do their job, and students enough credit to filter fact from opinion.

Lord knows, college professors are not getting paid all that much, and yet our campuses continue to attract dedicated teachers and leading researchers who see what they do as a kind of calling. It's a special thrill to them, to hand off what they know to a younger generation determined to know more of the same. The trade-off to the low salary, of course, is academic freedom, and contributing to the fulfillment of the students' hopes and dreams, and you can't put a price on that. Universities are the one place in the world where people have a chance to think outside the box a little bit, to come up with creative solutions to old problems. It's critical to our health as a society, to our strength and vision, and to our shared ability to put contemporary advances into historical context. Indeed, these very freedoms might one day yield some positive solutions to some of the problems plaguing our primary and secondary schools, so we'd do well not to curb any of them in the name of political correctness.

That said, our public universities are hamstrung in many of the same ways as other big institutions. There are layers and layers of bureaucracy. They're bound by unions and tenure, and entrenched in teaching models that in some cases are in desperate need of a facelift. And on top of everything else there's the constant worry over money. That's one of the things I think our bigtime universities have to watchdog carefully—the tug and pull in regard to money. Too often, university officials sell their souls in the name of fund-raising, or they overemphasize their intercollegiate athletic programs, which of course are a tremendous source of income as well as school pride. There's nothing wrong with having successful athletic programs, but you don't want your booster club having a say on the direction of your medical school. You don't want your enthusiasm for your football program to diminish your enthusiasm for a new science lab, because that starts to erode a school's foundation. And you certainly don't want to violate any of the recruiting rules put in place by the NCAA, or fall short in any of its academic standards, because that just puts a stain on the entire campus and throws the integrity of the administration into question.

BEYOND THE IVORY TOWER

Higher education is all about issues and ideas. I can think of no other place in our culture where people get paid to think, and it's a wonderful ideal, so much so that pioneers in every imaginable field find themselves daydreaming of the things they might accomplish in an academic setting. One of my closest friends, Mark Bechtal, is a doctor—the kind who still makes house calls, I should add—and he recently traded his medical practice for a second career as a professor. It was something he'd been meaning to do for the longest time. He had it all figured out, and when he laid out his plans for me one day while we were riding in the car I turned to him and said, "Mark, are you nuts?"

But he's not nuts, is he? He told me that he longs for the opportunity to work with medical students at the Arthur James Cancer Center on the Ohio State campus, coming up with new solutions to the problem of melanoma, conducting research, advancing new theories. He told me he'd have to take a hit in income, but he didn't even think of that as an issue. He was so passionate about teaching that when I got out of the car I called the dean and told him if he didn't hire this guy he was out of his mind, because my friend represents the best of what our universities have to offer.

And yet for every Mark Bechtal there's a Ward Churchill, or some other loose cannon who hides behind his tenure and abuses his position to advance his controversial views. Churchill, for those who missed these outrageous headlines in January 2005, was the chairman of the Ethnic Studies Department at the University of Colorado at Boulder, and a tenured professor there. His incendiary remarks, pulled from a 2001 essay on the September

Still, as the debate swirled around Ward Churchill I realized that such as this was a small toll to encourage open intellectual thought—and I reminded myself that we'd been paying the toll for generations. When I was a student, we had a professor at Ohio State who wondered aloud whether his students should toss rocks through the glass windows of the affluent homes in the area, in some sort of misguided protest against our well-heeled neighbors. I went to the vice president of student affairs and argued that this guy had to go, and after a couple weeks he was eventually fired—not because of me, I'm sure, but because he was a nut case, and tenure or no, the school wasn't obligated to keep a nut case on its payroll. At around the same time, our speakers bureau invited the political activist Angela Davis, an avowed Communist, to speak on campus, which I thought was just outrageous and offensive and unnecessary, not least because we were fighting a war that was ostensibly against Communism, but her appearance went off as planned, and I mention it here as a reminder that even unpopular opinions can find their place on our college campuses, then as now, and that students need to take in all kinds of viewpoints in order to formulate their own. It's when these unpopular views become inflammatory and hate-filled that I begin to have some trouble—and when they're underwritten by university funds, which in a way is tantamount to giving these inflammatory speakers the endorsement of university officials.

Here again, I'm astonished at the way some of us can't seem to learn from the missteps of others, because we're hardly through discussing the confrontational remarks of a Ward Churchill before we're made to consider the invective of another academic, off on his or her own tirade. Just a few weeks after the Churchill debate had faded from attention, there was a professor at Brooklyn College who touched off a great campus controversy by dismissing religious individuals as "an ugly, violent lot" and "moral retards." And—get this!—just a couple months later, the news hit about a university professor convicted on child sex abuse charges and still getting paid by the university because of his accrued vacation time, protected by their due process provisions for tenured professors. This last should not be tolerated by university administrators, because it threatens to undermine the legitimate reasons for tenure.

Even in the marketplace of ideas, justice and righteousness manage to prevail, and we should never lose sight of the fact that it is indeed a marketplace. Colleges and universities, public and private, go to great lengths to keep their market share—which in academic circles means that their classes remain fully enrolled, their dormitories filled, and their admissions offices inundated with enough applications from hopeful students that they can be selective in assembling each incoming class. Competition is key, across the board. College students have so many choices available to them that they're able to search for schools that offer the best fit, the newest facilities, the nicest campuses, the most dynamic professors, the richest opportunities in their intended fields of study. They can even shop the best deals, comparing financial aid packages or consider schools that do their best to keep costs under control over ones given to runaway spending.

THE BENEFITS OF COMPETITION

The reason America can boast the finest system of higher education in the world is because colleges and universities compete for the right to teach our children, and yet it's this very competition that's missing from our primary and secondary school system. The little red schoolhouses that sprang up in the eighteenth century are in desperate need of refurbishing, but there's no incentive to rebuild because the public school establishment has a kind of monopoly. I guess the thinking here is that as long as the building hasn't fallen down around them they're still in business, but there are too many cracks in the foundation at this point. Sure, there are an overwhelming number of dedicated, talented teachers out there, but I'm afraid that at the same time there are just too many substandard teachers who are allowed to keep their jobs because of tenure or complacency. Sure, there are private schools where the spirit of competition is alive and well, and more and more we're seeing families of means opt out of public schools in search of a more rigorous, more inspiring, more meaningful educational experience for their children, but many parents can't afford to make that kind of choice for their children. Why shouldn't every parent have the right to choose where their children go to school? Why shouldn't teachers have to compete for the right to educate students? Why is it that local politicians and school administrators are so petrified of the teachers' unions that they can't bring about change where change is needed most? That they allow teachers to hide behind tenure instead of holding them accountable?

Now, I'll shine that light on two of the glowing exceptions. I wrote briefly about the first in the opening pages of this book: the Frederick Douglass Academy, in New York City's Harlem, which stands in proud tribute to what a public school administration can accomplish by demanding excellence. From its teachers. From its students. From its entire community. This is a school that was shut down in the early 1980s because of excessive violence. It was located across the street from a crack house in one of the most depressed neighborhoods in the city. And yet it's been reopened and turned around on the back of an administration that believes strongly that students need to set the bar high for themselves in order to succeed, rededicated to the belief that excellence is an achievable goal. That there needs to be discipline and respect. That the front-burner question for high school kids should be, Where am I going to go to college?—and not, Where am I going to get my next fix?

Here's another shining example: a private high school in Jackson, Missouri, called Piney Woods Country Life School. It's run by a tremendous crusader for education reform named Charles Beady, and it caters mostly to students of low-income families that have been characterized as at-risk during their previous (and, for the most part, public) school careers. Like the Frederick Douglass Academy, Piney Woods demands excellence—and Charles Beady decided early on that firm discipline was essential to transforming at-risk youngsters into college-bound scholars. He developed his work ethic as a student himself, when his own father used to warn him not to bring home any Cs—"because they're as close to the bottom as they are to the top." Now, Piney Woods students are expected to dress neatly and work diligently. There are mandatory study halls. And all around the campus, posted on bulletin boards and signs and banners, is the school's slogan:

> *Fame Is Vapor*
> *Popularity an Accident*
> *Riches Take Wing*
> *Only One Thing Endures: Character!*

And the message has taken hold. Virtually all of Piney Woods graduates go on to college, many of them to prestige universities like Harvard and Princeton and to top black schools like Tuskegee, Grambling, and Morehouse—and every last one of them winds up closer to the top than the bottom, and I can't shake thinking that if we had a few thousand more principals like Charles Beady around the country we'd be doing a whole lot better on this score.

But I can shine a light on schools like Piney Woods and the Frederick Douglass Academy all day long, and it wouldn't change the fact that these are the exceptions. Both schools have unique models backed by the strength and vision of passionate, dedicated leaders. Both have accomplished great things by demanding that their students accomplish great things. Indeed, individuals can overcome models, but too often we find the model holding sway, and I can't for the life of me figure out why we cling so desperately to our tired old system.

Perhaps the most telling piece to the puzzle of public school education is that you can't throw money at the problem and expect it to go away. Increasing a school budget is no guarantee of success. In fact, some of our school districts with the highest rates of per-pupil spending post some of the worst results in statewide achievement and competency tests. How does that happen? Well, with God being thrown out of our schools, and discipline right along with Him, it's no wonder there's chaos in the classroom. I'm more comfortable putting my daughters in a school where they *can* talk about God or sing Christmas carols than I am consigning them to a school where they can't. That's how it was for me, in a public school setting. We read the Bible to start the day—the Old and New Testaments. Right there in class. We took turns. Try as I might, I still don't see what the harm is in acknowledging a higher power at the start of each day, but I guess I'm in the minority on this one.

I'll never forget one morning, just after we'd set aside our Bible reading and moved toward math, I was pulled aside by my teacher for talking to this pretty girl who had been seated in front of me. I guess I wasn't supposed to be talking, because the teacher hauled me off toward the back of the cloak room and swatted me on the backside with a paddle. And after he was through I looked at him and said, "I hope you don't tell my parents." That was my greatest fear, that my parents would punish me or ground me for one of these relatively benign transgressions, and it's amazing to me how far we've moved from those times. Realize, I'm not suggesting that the answer to our public school problems is to paddle our children, only that it would be a welcome development indeed if there was once again room enough in our classrooms for the kind of discipline that left kids more inclined to follow the Golden Rule than to blow the whistle on their teachers and threaten to call the family attorney if they're not left alone to do their thing—whatever it is that thing happens to be.

WHAT HAPPENED TO DISCIPLINE?

Paddling is a relic of the past, but it's amazing to me how far we've moved from the impulse behind it. In some academic circles, the debate doesn't even center on issues of discipline. It's *criticism* and *competition* that are at issue. Realize, the national Parent Teacher Association now suggests that school administrators outlaw playground games like tug-of-war in favor of more socially tolerant pastimes like tug-of-peace, and to deemphasize "threatening" activities like tag and dodgeball, which can create self-esteem issues in certain kids. Physical educators advocate activities through which children compete only with themselves, such as juggling, although even here it seems we need to offer a further assist in the interest of self-esteem; the President's Council on Physical Fitness and Sports recommends that gym teachers use scarves to teach juggling skills because they're so much more forgiving (and easier to juggle) than tennis balls or bean bags.

There's even a movement among classroom teachers to promote the use of kinder, gentler colors like purple and green when grading papers, setting aside the proverbial red pen in favor of muted tones intended to have a more calming influence on our children.

I look on at such as this and think, What the heck is going on here? Surely, children who are protected from the sting of honest, constructive criticism can't hope to compete with their counterparts around the world where educators are free to push kids to achieve their level best. Surely, kids can meet the high expectations of their teachers without being coddled. We can protect them all we like from stressful situations, disappointments, and threats to their self-esteem, but in the long run is it really in their best interest to paint everything in such pleasant-feeling tones?

Still, the opportunity for discipline remains. What is discipline anyway but a negative consequence or a series of negative consequences or the threat of negative consequences intended to curb bad behavior? In a private school setting, the ultimate consequence is expulsion; in a public school setting, you get suspended; and the answer to some of the more garden-variety behavioral problems lies somewhere in between.

Remember that story, not too long ago, where students recorded footage of a teacher blowing his top at the unruly behavior in his classroom with the camcorder feature on their cell phones? It made the rounds of all the news shows and Web sites for the way it demonstrated how easy it was for certain students to push the buttons of certain teachers—and to very often get their way as a result, to see the teacher disciplined instead of the student. Mercifully, the school ended up backing the teacher in this one case, and refused to consider the video footage showing the teacher as something less than cool and calm and professional, but it was nevertheless a distressing reminder how much power students have in today's classrooms. Goodness, you've got schools catering to kids who cause trouble, and precious little support for the teachers, and administrators who reach into their bags of tricks to cover up for the weaknesses in their school districts, and it's no wonder we're struggling.

DOLLARS AND SENSE

For too long now, the rallying cry among public school educators has been that if they just had enough money they could fix the problem. Aw, give me a break! Money is not going to fix the problems endemic to our primary and secondary system of public education any more than a fresh coat of paint for our little red schoolhouses—and we do our kids a great disservice when we hide behind this argument. Too, we miss the point when we pin it all on the parents, by suggesting the problems in our schools would melt away if the parents were more involved in their kids' schooling. Absolutely, teachers would have an easier time of it if parents weren't so blind to what was going on in their classrooms, just as they would have an easier time if parents didn't blindly support their kids in every student-teacher conflict. Absolutely, our parents are not involved in the ways they need to be to reinforce achievement at home. For the most part, they don't have a clue. They send their kids off to school with no more thought than sending them down to the local barbershop to get a haircut, and they expect them to return all spit-shined and polished and ready to meet the challenges that lie in wait, but it requires more of a hands-on effort, don't you think? It means parents might need to take those televisions and video game players out of their children's bedrooms and pay closer attention to the work they're meant to be doing. It means parents must be willing to give over a certain amount of authority to educators in their communities, while continuing to hold those educators accountable for that authority.

There's an adversarial relationship in place these days, between teachers and parents, and it ought to be more of a partnership. That said, it's not *just* on the parents any more than it is *just* on the teachers, or the administrators, or the elected officials charged with the care and feeding of our public school systems. The irony here is that when parents do get involved they frequently bump up against teachers and administrators who don't know how to handle them, but parents must persevere in this area—as partners and as quality-conscious consumers. Once, when I was out in California, I was riding in a cab through a local community and noticed a long line of well-dressed, well-mannered adults that seemed to stretch for several blocks. I asked the driver to stop, and I walked over to talk to the people in line, to find out what was going on. (I was running for president at the time, and this is the sort of thing presidential candidates are inclined to do.)

I asked the first person in line who made eye contact with me what they were doing, and I learned they'd been queued up for hours, hoping to get a spot for their children in a new charter school program that was to begin the following school year. Then I walked to the very back of the line and asked the woman standing in the last spot what she would do if she reached the front of the line and learned there was no longer any room for her child. "There are only so many spaces," I said.

She couldn't imagine that would happen, she said, and I thought, Oh, yes it will. She, or someone in line, would get to the door and it would slam shut and there'd be a sign dangling from the window saying, "Sorry, sold out," like she'd been waiting on line for tickets to a show. She'd have done what she could, and meanwhile her kid, her flesh and blood, her future, would be denied an opportunity to truly learn and flourish in a landmark school environment

I came away thinking we have no choice but to open up all of our schools in just this way, so that we can finally put some teeth into the "No Child Left Behind" mantra that passes for an education policy these days, and if we can't give parents full choice on the education of their own children then we ought to at least fight for a robust charter school movement. There's a rousing example of a charter school in Las Vegas, funded by the tennis player Andre Agassi, where the school day runs eight hours instead of the traditional six. "That's a third more time on task," notes Agassi, who opened the school in 2001 in hopes of giving something back to his home community, and providing a blueprint for how charter schools might flourish in other parts of the country. That two-hour difference each day might not seem like much, Agassi notes, "but at the end of an education, instead of going to twelve years of school, you're going to sixteen years of school."

It's that kind of outside-the-box thinking that will shake some of the dust from our primary and secondary school models and leave our children in a better position to compete in a global marketplace of ideas. Already, the Andre Agassi College Preparatory Academy, which expects to graduate its first class in 2009 and where admission is done by lottery, boasts a waiting list of more than three hundred children, so in at least one neglected neighborhood in at least one of our booming metropolitan communities, we see that the charter school movement can work—in a big way, by combining public and private monies with a little bit of ingenuity and progressive new approaches.

VOICES OF REASON

We ought to find some way to inject competition into a tired, rickety system and see if that doesn't help, because competition drives everything in our society. Better computers. Better cars. Better medicine. Better opportunities. Better everything. And yet the powers that be have decided that in this one area there will be no such thing. It's like the airline industry, where the barriers to entry were such that for the longest time there was no real competition; the giant airlines lumbered along under the constraints of federal regulators that left them with no good reason to innovate—and so, they didn't. Along came Southwest Airlines, and other short-hop, regional carriers, and a relaxing of some of those regulations, and all of a sudden these upstarts had reinvented the wheel. They figured out how to take care of the customer, how to keep labor costs in check, how to break the mold and look at the tired, rickety ways of doing business from a fresh perspective. And we've all benefited from it—with more efficient, more affordable service.

Over time, we'll see some of the same benefits in our public schools, I'm sure of it, if we find a way to harness that same spirit of competition and put it to work for our children. Trouble is, we're running out of time. This is another one of those areas where things have got to go horribly wrong before they've got a chance to go haltingly right, and the way I look at it we're well past horribly wrong. We're well past the point when some group or individual needs to rise above the mess and demand proactive change, and I'm afraid it's not going to be the parents, and it's not going to be the school administrators, and it's not going to be the politicians, and it's certainly not going to be the students. That leaves the teachers. Imagine the powerful message our teachers could send if they simply threw up their hands and said, "This is a farce." Imagine the strength of that kind of argument, because who knows better than our teachers that our public system of primary and secondary school education is simply not working? They know it firsthand and full well.

Imagine in your own hometown what would happen if a group of teachers stood united against the low standards of your school, if they walked out in protest, and contacted the media, and otherwise called attention to a systemic problem we've looked away from for far too long. What would happen? Well, I'll tell you one thing: Those teachers would never be fired. The administration would be so paralyzed it wouldn't know how to respond, and parents would lend their voice to the protest, and soon enough something would be done about it. I'm not suggesting that we organize these spontaneous protests all across the country to bring about these much needed reforms, but the power of one such act—one school, one place, one time, one stand—would be enormous, don't you think?

I've got no idea where it might take us, but it would be a start.

8

TAKING A STAND
ON POPULAR CULTURE

"I wouldn't have turned out the way I was if I didn't
have all those old-fashioned values to rebel against."

Madonna

*Janet Jackson flashes her breast during the halftime show at
Super Bowl XXXVIII—one of the most watched broad-
casts in television history—and later blames a "wardrobe
malfunction" for her state of undress as sales of her new
album soar . . .*

*Comedian Bill Maher, who had already been chased from
ABC's late night schedule when he argued on his Politically Incorrect talk show in September 2001 that the ter-
rorists who flew the planes into the World Trade Center
were not "cowards," now suggests on his HBO Real Time
program that the U.S. military has picked all the "low-lying
fruit" from our inner cities and rural areas and will continue to fall short of its recruiting goals . . .*

Lifestyle expert Martha Stewart resurfaces after five months in a federal prison in West Virginia, for lying to federal investigators, and another five months under house arrest, and announces she will star in an NBC prime-time television show, in a deal that was struck while she was incarcerated . . .

Ozzy Osbourne, a founding father of heavy metal whose dark, satanic music with Black Sabbath purportedly influenced hundreds of impressionable teenagers to contemplate suicide, and whose onstage antics included biting off the heads of live chickens, allows MTV to film his dysfunctional family for an expletive-laced reality television series, and emerges as a lovable, irascible "sitcom dad" whose drinking and drug use have merely left him unable to find his car keys . . .

It's enough to make you cringe, isn't it? Anyway, it does me, and try as MTV might, I will never be able to snicker at Ozzy Osbourne's years of excessive and reckless behavior—an inside joke that I guess is over my level head. I will never get that our celebrity transgressions carry no real consequences to the transgressor; indeed, they often return a substantive windfall, in the form of a book deal, a television show, a commercial, or a rejuvenated public image. I will never accept that disorder has become the order of the day. I will never understand how yesterday's R movies have become today's PG fare, and how what used to be unthinkable on prime-time network television is now so pervasive that most of us don't even think about it. I will never stop seeking the national conscience that ought to lie beneath everything that passes for entertainment.

And so I cringe instead, at the general coarsening of America's ethical standards, and when I'm done cringing I get to wondering if I've become so out of touch with the mores and manners of our popular culture that my own standards come across as old-fashioned. Or maybe it's that the lines of acceptable behavior have been so radically redrawn over the last couple generations that I'm left toeing the traditional lines of my growing up, trying to figure when it was that the world passed me by. But then I check myself and think, Heck, Kasich, you're not *that* old, and your world hasn't changed *that* much; it's just that my perspective has changed, as I've taken on the role of father, and what was once acceptable (or, hardly worth noticing) suddenly looms as all-important. And it's not just me. There are millions of young-at-heart parents out there and they're probably cut a lot like me on this one, wondering how to stand against the constant bombardment of negative messages that now permeate the popular culture. We've all been caught napping, while our standards have slipped to where they no longer seem to be standards at all, and our kids have been left to essentially figure things out for themselves.

Britney Spears and Madonna leave off writhing onstage long enough to lock lips at the MTV Video Music Awards, in a steamy kiss that raises more than a few eyebrows in the increasingly uninhibited entertainment industry and sends shock waves across the American heartland . . .

I'll tell you how old I am: I can still remember the first time the Beatles appeared on *The Ed Sullivan Show*. My, what a fuss we made over these British imports—in McKees Rocks, and across the country. It was all anyone seemed to want to talk about, the end of civilization as we knew it, in much the same way Elvis and his gyrating hips had marked our decline just a few years earlier. My parents weren't exactly aghast or put out when the Beatles burst onto the scene and into our living rooms, but in our household these guys were almost counterculture, with the noise everyone in the media was making about their long hair, and their rock 'n' roll music, and the raw adulation heaped on them by their female fans. This is what I mean by perspective, because nowadays of course we look back on the Beatles as a mostly positive phenomenon, and apart from their very public experimentation with drugs their musical influence turned out mostly to our great and lasting benefit, but back then there was a sense among my parents' generation that they were up to no good.

Everything is relative, I guess, and perspective is all, so when we look at these various sea changes in our popular culture we have to be careful that we're not merely resistant to change. And that we don't come across as old fogies. That's about the last image I want to put out about myself, and I'm betting that most of my readers feel the same way regarding their own views. In my case, I'm about as plugged in to the latest trends in music and movies and fashion as any other old fogy in my acquaintance. I know full well that times change, and that our tastes change right along with them, and I've been pretty good over the years, trying to stay on top of each, and I recognize that we have become a society of extremes. What is Ashton Kutcher's *Punk'd*, after all, but a more provocative version of Allen Funt's *Candid*

Camera? And what are any of our contemporary entertainments but more provocative versions of the books, movies, music, and television shows that inspired them? Everything old is new again—but unfortunately we live in a time when everything must be new *and* improved *and* more sensational than ever before, and I don't know that we're coming out ahead on the deal.

WALKING THAT WHOLESOME ROAD

There's a thinking out there, in Hollywood and other centers of the entertainment industry, that the G-rated fare of yesterday won't fly in today's R-rated world, but a recent study puts this argument flat on its face. The Dove Foundation, a group that encourages the production of family-friendly movies, studied the gross earnings of the two hundred most widely distributed studio films each year from 1989 to 2003. Not surprisingly, slightly more than half of those films (or, 51.4 percent) received an R rating from the Motion Picture Association of America. PG-13 movies came next, at 28.4 percent, followed by PG movies, at 16.1 percent. Trailing the field, by a wide margin, were G-rated titles, representing only 4.1 percent of all major studio releases during that period.

But here's the shocker: G-rated movies raked in an average profit of $79 million, while R-rated movies managed an average profit of only $6.9 million, putting to lie the myth that family-friendly fare doesn't make money—and sending out an all-important reminder to entertainment executives that Americans seem to be hungering for movies and music and television shows they can enjoy wholeheartedly with their children.

Realize, I don't come at this argument from any kind of sidelong view. I watched MTV when it was first getting off the ground back in the early 1980s, and I still watch it today—only lately I start in with my cringing a little sooner than I ever did before. To be sure, there was gratuitous sex and violence in a lot of those early music videos, but it's become much more hard-core in recent years, and much more disturbing, to where I can no longer look away from it. I still listen to new music, but more and more these days I find there are some thresholds I have a hard time crossing. I bought the new Roots CD, for example, be-cause I try to stay on top of things, and because I was determined to give hip-hop a fair shake. It's hard to ignore it, because even if I turn the dial it pops up on the next station. It's everywhere, and all around, so I slipped in this new CD and was quickly ap-palled at what I was hearing. The lyrics just put me over the edge. Every other word, or just about, was intended to shock and titillate, for no good reason but to shock and titillate, and I couldn't listen to it.

I'm not a moralizer, and I like to think I have an open mind, but I've got to tell you I couldn't open it wide enough to accept such as this, and as I listened to the CD I kept coming back to the language. I won't repeat any of it here, but it was so unre-lentingly foul and offensive, almost gratuitously so, that I caught myself feeling angry at myself for even listening. More than that, I was angry that I was being subjected to it. Realize, it wasn't so foul and offensive that I became morally outraged or anything like that, but I couldn't see the point. The language didn't add anything to the music, or to the message, which I guess is the very definition of *gratuitous*. And then I caught my-self thinking, What if my wife got in the car and the album hap-pened to still be in my CD changer? How could I ever explain what I was doing buying this stuff? Or, even worse, what if my daughters chanced to hear it? How could I ever explain to them why Daddy was listening to such filth? There was no justifying it, really, and yet I suppose on balance it was little different from any other rap or hip-hop artist out there making music today. It's what we've become, in our society of extremes, and what we've tacitly agreed to accept, as we vote with our dollars and ratings, and there I was on the consumer end of the equation, embarrassed to be a part of it.

So what did I do? I pulled into this place near my house where I usually stop for coffee and threw the CD in the trash. I didn't even think it through, just pulled up alongside this garbage can, popped the CD from the console, and threw it away. Understand, I never throw anything in the trash like that, but I was so put off by what I'd heard that it seemed the only thing to do. The right thing to do. In my own way, I was taking my own little stand, against the societal drift we've allowed ourselves to get caught up in, against the meaningless and increasingly offensive drivel that passes for intellectual or creative thought. We throw up our hands like we're powerless against it, but in truth there is tremendous power even in a small act such as this, which struck me at just that moment as all-important. Why? Because I couldn't believe that these talented artists would obscure their gifts with such vulgarity by their own choosing. Because I couldn't believe that I had spent my hard-earned money to listen to it. And because I'd convinced myself that if I let that kind of garbage into my life and the life of my family I'd have lost—and yet even as I slipped back into my car I worried this was yet another case of too little, too late. We've all lost, really, in big ways and small, because this kind of garbage is everywhere and all around, and I maintain that if we don't stand against it, if we don't take our own little stands, we'll look up one day and it will be who we are.

> *Paris Hilton doubles-down for another fifteen minutes of fame by agreeing to videotape a sex act with her boyfriend and laughs it off when the footage becomes the most popular download on the Internet—and laughs harder still when she becomes one of the most popular personalities on the celebrity scene, parlaying her "home movies" into a hit reality show, a best-selling book, a successful clothing line, a guest-hosting gig on* Saturday Night Live, *and a suggestive commercial for a fast food hamburger chain . . .*

Ours has become a culture of celebrity, wouldn't you agree? We've got actors and musicians passing themselves off as environmental experts and political analysts, stumping for this or that cause or candidate, and we've allowed their opinions to influence our own—all because of the power of their celebrity. We've got rap artists like 50 Cent, making the rounds to promote his debut CD, proudly telling admiring interviewers on mainstream news and talk shows that he'd been shot so many times in his young life it's a wonder he doesn't leak. We've got music videos that denigrate women and glorify violence, and reality shows that encourage contestants to eat the stir-fried phalluses of yaks, and video games that cast players in the role of a disaffected student off to shoot up his high school. All in the name of entertainment.

And, like it or not, we've got Paris Hilton, who in the blink of a false eyelash has become *the* pop icon of her generation—for no valid reason I can easily determine. Okay, so she comes from a rich family, and we seem to want to catch her behaving badly, but that should be where it begins and ends for this young woman. How is it that we've managed to build her up into such a name-above-the-title-type star that she shines brighter than the signature H outside her family's hotels? There's no talent here, at least none that I can see. For all I know, Paris Hilton is whip-smart and has strategically crafted a public persona—a *brand*, in today's parlance—that will serve her enormously well in the years ahead; at the very least, she's smart enough to have surrounded herself with whip-smart advisors. But beyond the marketing blitz, there's no personality, no great charisma, no undeniable charm. She's a pretty girl, is all, and judging by her scandalous behavior she's pretty much willing to do anything, and this last has been enough to push her onto the cover of every popular magazine in the country. I don't mean to rip Paris Hilton, because I've never met her and I've tried diligently to avoid her "work," and I don't mean to dwell on her rise to such prominence because I don't want to give it any more attention than it deserves. But I think her appeal is emblematic. There's no *there* there, and yet she is absolutely everywhere, and I can't be quite sure if the public has embraced her as much as her handlers would have us believe, or if the media haven't foisted her upon us and left us with no choice in the matter.

WHY CELEBRITY MATTERS

I understand our fascination with wealth. I get the appeal of shows like *Lifestyles of the Rich and Famous*—or, these days, MTV's *Cribs*. They play to our prurient interest, and speak to that part of us that's always thinking the grass is somehow greener on the other side of the fence. I'll sometimes watch these shows myself, because I like seeing how rich people spend their money, how many fancy cars they have in their driveways, how elaborate they've made their home gymnasiums or screening rooms. This kind of stuff is interesting to people, in a Peeping Tom sort of way, but it's when we put these celebrities on a kind of altar and begin to worship at it that we get ourselves into trouble, because it's one thing to check out how *they* live and quite another to have it influence how *we* live.

And the most troubling piece is that, in the main, our celebrities are clearly not up to the position, because a great many of them seem to get themselves into trouble at every turn. We've given them the burden of shouldering our expectations, and modeling our behavior, but what comes back to us on the rebound is one scandal after another, each one more notorious than the last:

> *Halle Berry, the Oscar-winning actress, is convicted for leaving the scene of an automobile accident, and sentenced to 200 hours of community service and three years' probation . . .*
>
> *Paul Reubens, better known as children's entertainer Pee-wee Herman, is caught exposing himself in an adult theater in Florida . . .*
>
> *Hugh Grant, one of Hollywood's most popular leading men, is arrested for soliciting a prostitute in Los Angeles . . .*

> *R. Kelly, the Grammy-winning R&B singer-songwriter whose hit "I Believe I Can Fly" became an inspiring anthem for inner city youth looking to harness their dreams, is indicted on child pornography counts in Cook County, Illinois, as his new album goes multiplatinum . . .*
>
> *Winona Ryder, another acclaimed movie star, is arrested for shoplifting $5,500 in clothing from the Beverly Hills Saks Fifth Avenue . . .*

Once again, it begs the question: What the heck are these people thinking? And, the too easy follow-up: Are they even thinking at all? I feel the same way about these misguided celebrities as I do about our athletes, and it's amazing to me that they can have so much going for them—looks, talent, wealth, fame—and still be determined to throw it all away on the back of a bad decision. And, as often as not, it's not just one bad decision, but one after another. I read about their various falls from grace and start to think, Why don't these celebrities use their powers for good? Why don't they turn their popularity to advantage and build on the public interest to shine important or compelling light on one thing or another? Why don't they use their positions of influence and authority to actually stand for something?—something *positive*, that is.

Of course, the stars are not solely to blame for their various inabilities to lead purposeful, value-laden lives away from stage and screen; it's also on the industries in which they toil. And it's on us. Flip around the television dial and you'll get what I mean, as you come across show after show laced with sexual innuendo and senseless violence. Even at seven and eight o'clock at night, there's stuff on network television I certainly wouldn't want my daughters watching. Goodness, I couldn't even begin to explain away some of what passes for acceptable behavior on some of these shows! The comedian George Carlin used to do a routine about the seven dirty words you couldn't say on television, and I won't stoop to repeat them here, but I will state that I've since heard most of them on prime-time network shows. And the ones I haven't heard have been hinted at.

THE SLIPPERY SLOPE

When did it happen that you were allowed to show partial nudity on network television? When did it happen that the story lines of shows scheduled in what used to be known as the eight o'clock "family hour" included such subjects as sexual promiscuity, unprotected sex, bisexuality, and group sex? When did it happen that sexual innuendo became the default option programmed into the hard drives of Hollywood's so-called comedy writers? And when, pray tell, did it become acceptable to treat hot-button issues like abortion, single motherhood, and same-sex marriage so cavalierly that they can be delivered with a laugh track? Our young people are especially vulnerable to the kind of idol worship that leaves them mimicking the behavior of their favorite characters and stars, and we're fooling ourselves into thinking they can take in all these mixed messages and begin to make sense of them. Forget the off-camera exploits of some of these celebrities—it's the on-camera scenes that create such a disturbing impression. It's the willingness of Hollywood producers to set aside conscience and promote all manner of irresponsible messages to our impressionable young people that gets us into trouble—and keeps us there, for the near term. Why is it that writers are so quick to romanticize, say, the plight of an unwed teenage mother? Ask them about it and they'll say it sends an empowering message, to demonstrate to young female viewers that it's possible for an intelligent, strong-willed, independent woman to go it alone as a single mother. They'll say it's a creative choice, well within their purview as writers and entertainers. That would be their view, and they'd be entitled to it, but I look on and think it's a missed opportunity to address the root social ills of teenage and unwed pregnancies.

Say what you will about Hollywood producers, but the best-intentioned of them realize that we live in a global village, and that as producers of popular entertainments that coarsen our society they have a deleterious impact on our children and consequently our future, thereby lowering our societal bar. They don't produce this stuff in a vacuum; there's a consequential cause and effect at work here. I don't care where you fit in Hollywood's pecking order, just to continue with this one example, whether you're an actor, or a writer, or a grip . . . everyone bears responsibility for the finished product and for the insidious effect it might have on our society. Even parents are responsible, because they're the gatekeepers of last resort, capable of shutting this stuff off and keeping it from their children—in most instances.

Like it or not, we mimic our fictional heroes and heroines, just as we mimic our real-life heroes and heroines, and if a brassy, determined female character happens to stand as a role model to millions of American women, the people who created that character have a certain obligation to present her in a positive, hopeful manner. Does that mean that each and every one of our recurring television characters must always be made to act morally and responsibly? Does it mean our best-selling novelists must only create protagonists who demonstrate positive ideals? Does it mean rap artists must only write songs about peace and love and helping others? Absolutely not, because that would be boring, but if we're going to have a popular character embrace a "lifestyle choice" in a meaningful and lasting way, then we had better think it through because our kids are watching, and reading over our shoulders, and making their own choices based on these so-called creative decisions.

A recent RAND Corporation study brings the point powerfully home, revealing that teens who watch a lot of television with sexual content are more likely to initiate intercourse in the following year than teens who don't. In effect, the study showed, young Americans who watch the most television with sexual content "act older" than their peers who watch less. They have intercourse at an earlier age. The silver lining is that television shows addressing the risks of sexual promiscuity, or discussing some of the consequences of that promiscuity, tend to have a positive impact on our children, who are more likely to practice safe sex as a result of having seen one of their favorite characters practice safe sex on television, but I see that only as a silver lining to a mess of dark clouds.

> ABC-TV *airs a titillating promo for its hit show* Desperate Housewives, *as a lead-in to its* Monday Night Football *broadcast. The spot features actress Nicolette Sheridan, one of the attractive stars of the show, dressed only in a tight-fighting bath towel, crossing an otherwise empty NFL locker room toward Philadelphia Eagles wide receiver Terrell Owens, and as the camera pulls close she suggestively*

> *drops her towel. The network is flooded with calls of protest from angry parents and watchdog groups who argue that the spot was irresponsible, and inappropriate, and the network issues a public apology the next morning . . .*

Enough's enough, don't you think? I mean, network television executives ought to know better than to put this kind of provocative imagery on its prime-time airwaves, at the front end of a broadcast when millions of adolescent boys are sitting down to watch the game with their fathers, and yet somehow it passes muster with enough suits and knee-jerk executives that it winds up in our homes—and this is what I find so unacceptable. Once again, I'm not such an old prude to suggest that the sight of an attractive actress in a bath towel is the end of the world, or that the suggestion that she is about to walk naked across a men's locker room to seduce a nearly naked football player is patently offensive—but in this context it was definitely out of place, and ill-conceived, and it leaves me thinking we ought to be doing a better job policing ourselves on this type of thing. I'm not arguing for a return to censorship but I am calling for a redoubling of self-censorship on the part of network executives. Let's start paying attention to these types of improprieties and figure some of this stuff out for ourselves, because I find it hard to believe that each and every network suit who signed off on this *Desperate Housewives* promotional spot didn't see this one coming. It wasn't a decision made in a vacuum; it was a decision made by a committee, and any committee worth its six-figure bonus should have known that such a lewd, suggestive spot was bound to backfire—especially when parents have a quite reasonable expectation that when their children tune in to an NFL football game they won't be assaulted with such as this. The constant barrage of negative images ought to at least be limited to the bad behavior demonstrated by the athletes on the field.

Violence. Coarse behavior. An erosion of the family structure. Glorification of premarital sex and recreational drug abuse. It's all fair game to music video directors, and television producers, and screenwriters, and video game designers—and even to clothing designers and fashion magazine editors who convince our impressionable young children that it's okay to go to school with their belly buttons exposed, or their underwear showing from their low-hanging jeans, or their noses pierced and connected to their ears with a sterling chain. I maintain that we need to take some of this stuff off the table. It's like my friend Bobby Kotick at Activision, making socially responsible video games and avoiding the shoot-'em-up, blood-and-guts filth that fills the toy aisles, even if it costs his publicly traded company an all-important segment of his business. We need to pull back, and realize that if we can't make a positive contribution to our shared template of socially acceptable behavior with each and every creative choice then we should at least try—to do better, to balance each piece of hopelessness with an extra piece of hope, to look for ways to celebrate our ideals. Go ahead and write the story line about the unwed mother, or the teenage prostitute, or the deadbeat dad, or publish the video game that awards points for gunning down cops from the window of your tricked-out sports car, but look for ways to counter these negatives with a positive every now and then, because when you work in these powerful mediums you've got a tremendous platform, and along with it a tremendous responsibility to model appropriate behavior. Don't take it lightly.

It comes down to taking sides, just as it does in the world of sports—just as it does, really, in every aspect of American society. As responsible, moral adults, we must ask ourselves which team we want to be on, and where we want to align ourselves when it comes to these pop culture indicators. Do we side with the anything-goes-types who sink as low as our standards and practices allow, all the while looking to push those standards and practices ever lower? Or do we look to trod some higher ground, demanding entertainments that are at least rooted in decency?

> *Students at the University of Maryland embrace a single swear word as their all-purpose chant at school basketball games, showering the F-word down on opposing players, shouting it out for the sheer joy of it, or donning T-shirts featuring "F— You!" as its slogan. It becomes such a pervasive aspect of home games that ESPN officials lodge a formal protest against the school, out of fear that it could not responsibly air a Maryland game beneath the swirl of such profanity, while school administrators refuse to eject offending students from the game, or to take disciplinary action against them . . .*

Absolutely, role modeling is important. It influences our national behavior, and sets an all-important tone, and the sophomoric swearing of college students is emblematic of the trend to "vile down" the culture in response to the increasingly vile impulses that permeate the pop culture scene.

THE COSBY IMPERATIVE

Here's just one example of how we might stand against the negative images that prevail in our movies, and video games, and music videos: No less a role model than Bill Cosby, the veteran comedian who in recent years has become an advocate for contemporary African-American culture, set off a national debate by criticizing blacks in our poorest communities for not doing enough to right their own situation. In language that bounced from harsh to humorous to humane, Cosby was openly critical of blacks who fail to accept personal responsibility and choose instead to blame a predominantly white society for their disadvantages and misfortunes. In a speech before the NAACP, he said, "*Brown versus the Board of Education* is no longer the white person's problem. We have got to take the neighborhood back. We have to go in there, forget about telling your child to go into the Peace Corps, it is right around the corner. [Our children] are standing on the corner and they can't speak English."

He continued, railing against "millionaire" basketball players who "can't write a paragraph" and football players who "can't read": "Yes, *Brown versus the Board of Education* paved the way, but where are we today? What did we do with it? That white man, he's laughing. He's got to be laughing. Fifty percent of [our children] drop out. The rest of them are in prison."

Cosby's comments took America by surprise, coming as they did from someone who was accustomed to making us laugh instead of making us think, and his position infuriated a great many leaders in the black community, but that's why his message was so powerful. He dared to articulate an unpopular view in order to bring about change, and in the fallout set in motion a kind of crusade to bring that message to anyone who might have missed his NAACP speech. "It is not all right for your fifteen-year-old daughter to have a child," he admonished an audience of about two thousand in a Milwaukee high school. And he shocked another thousand or so fans in an Atlanta audience by criticizing single mothers for having sex within their children's hearing—"and then four days later you bring another man into the house." In another appearance, he blasted "lower-economic people" for buying their kids $500 sneakers instead of "Hooked on Phonics."

Unfortunately (although, perhaps, predictably), Cosby has been ridiculed and attacked for his comments, and I imagine it will cost him over the long haul, in terms of his concert ticket sales or his Q rating, but I think it showed tremendous character to stand up and take on his entire community. He's standing up, and being heard, and voicing a view that for too long people have been unwilling to put into words. All that great comedy he did over the years means nothing to me compared to what he's saying here. And, man, is he taking heat. I look on and think, Good for him—that he has the courage to stand behind his words, and the wisdom to recognize that as an educated black man with a gigantic following that cuts across all racial, social, and economic boundaries, he's probably one of the few people in America in a position to vent on an issue like this.

And, so, he vents, and as we listen in we remind ourselves that we've all got to help with the heavy lifting, in what ways we can, and that it falls to each of us to take responsibility, to be a voice of reason, to lead so that others might follow. Why is it that no one else with Bill Cosby's stature has taken such a firm stand—on this or any other compelling social issue? Why is it that when they do stick their necks out and voice appropriate concern, people like Bill Cosby have to pay for it by becoming the butt of one of Jay Leno's jokes on the *Tonight* show? It's no wonder, I guess, that these people are hiding, but if we mean to set America right they need to take the lead in this area, and share their principled views, and hope to get a hearing.

Indeed, anyone can find himself in a position of power or influence, but it's the individual who uses that position of power or influence for the greater good who can truly claim the mantle of leader.

> *Schoolteacher Mary Kay Letourneau is imprisoned for having sex with her twelve-year-old student Vili Fualaau, but continues her pursuit of the young man and eventually marries him when she leaves prison nearly ten years later. The wedding is attended by the couple's two children, and covered exclusively by* Entertainment Tonight *and* The Insider, *wherein producers refer to this unseemly relationship as a "unique love story" . . .*
>
> *Jayson Blair, the* New York Times *reporter charged with fabricating stories and plagiarizing materials, is rewarded for his transparent lack of journalistic ethics with a six-figure book deal . . .*

A word or two on the media, which also acts as a gatekeeper in this regard, and in some respects feeds the systemic abuse of power and moral bankruptcy that permeates our culture. I don't mean to group the above two items in such a way as to suggest that the *New York Times* is in the same category as *Entertainment*

Tonight and *The Insider* and other infotainment-type celebrity news programs, but I believe our tabloid television producers share many of the same responsibilities as our leading journalists. Taken together, they set our national agenda, and hold a mirror to who we are and how we behave—and, depending on the angle of that mirror, we take what we want from the reflection. They ought to get the story right, and report it fairly, and responsibly. There's no room in the mainstream media for an agenda of any kind, whether you're Dan Rather and CBS News reporting that President Bush was given preferential treatment in his National Guard service, or Court TV offering up purported insight and analysis of Michael Jackson's child molestation trial. Let us never forget the power of the printed word or the weight of a broadcast report, because Americans rely on all these sources of information and regard them as truth, but at the same time let us never forget that readers and ratings drive virtually every news-related decision in every newsroom in this country. These numbers are like gravity—in the news business, as in any other. They're a fact of life. But there's got to be some conscience underneath the numbers or we'll lose our footing.

To offer an example from personal experience, I know that on my own FOX News show we must sometimes devote time to stories that appeal to our base instincts. I'm not thrilled that I must spend half my show covering, say, the saga of Jennifer Wilbanks, the Georgia woman who skipped out on her wedding in Spring 2005, but I know the reality of my business, and I look to find a balance. Hopefully, you don't just do what feeds the beast, but you offer stories and insights that give people a chance to learn something new. On our show, we've done stories on the United Nations, Sudan, Ukraine . . . before any other mainstream show would touch these topics, because I feel duty-bound to shine a light in as many corners of the world as possible. And do you know what? These stories are "rating," as we say in our newsroom—which means folks in the heartland are tuning in.

IT'S NEWS TO US

The real question journalists of every stripe should be asking is, "Am I pimping this story or am I reporting this story?" There's wide latitude in terms of what you say and write, just as there's great freedom in deciding which stories you'll cover in the first place. I think back to the great legacy of Franklin Delano Roosevelt, and wonder if he could have won reelection as president in today's political climate, under the intense glare of our modern media. At the time, the nature of FDR's health and the extent of his disability due to polio were never fully reported in the press, and he was propped up before the crowds and the cameras in such a way that the American public never had a true sense of his condition. They knew, but at the same time they didn't *know*, because the media back then chose to emphasize FDR's strengths as a leader over his physical weakness as a man. Today, I'm guessing, there'd be note and comment from his nurses and doctors and designers of the presidential wheelchair, with voters left knowing everything there was to know about their disabled leader, and the contrast begs the question: Was it *responsible* for American journalists to sweep so much about FDR's condition under the rug—in a time of war, as he faced reelection? And, the inevitable follow-up question: Is it *responsible* for today's journalists to dig out so much dirt from beneath all kinds of rugs that they keep good candidates from even seeking office?

There are no easy answers to these questions, but I do know this: We ought to be thankful for our free press. It's not a perfect system, and everywhere you look there are abuses of it, but it's our salvation. It's sort of like politics, and religion, and business. We look on and see things we don't like, and yet we recognize what we have and make the most of it, and it's in making the most of it that we stand apart. It's what keeps us honest, and moving forward. The leaders in the media can raise the bar, and stand for something, in many of the same ways as the celebrated men and women to whom they devote their front-burner attention, thereby advancing our general condition. They can inform, enlighten, and expand our horizons. Or, they can drag us into the gutter and encourage us to rubberneck as our misguided celebrities make one misstep after another.

It's on them, and it's on us, and it takes us back one final time to the daddy-cam or mommy-cam concept I advocated early on in these pages. We'll get it right eventually, if we can simply manage to conduct ourselves as if our children are watching—at all times, in all things. Because they are. And, because they will keep on watching until we do get it right, at which point we will finally be able to look away and know we've given them the tools they need to get it right for themselves.

9

TAKING THE NEXT STEP

"Peace is normally a great good, and normally it coincides with righteousness, but it is righteousness and not peace which should bind the conscience of a nation as it should bind the conscience of an individual; and neither a nation nor an individual can surrender conscience to another's keeping."

Theodore Roosevelt

Setting right the American pendulum is not about venting. If it were, we'd all be hoarse from talking our own blue streaks—and deaf from tuning out the rants of our friends and neighbors. Venting is a part of it, to be sure, and it might even play a central role from time to time, but we need more than mere talk in order to bring about change. We need action. And we need leadership. I've been calling for a healthy dose of each throughout these pages, and I'll sound the call one final time here, because leadership is *doing*.

To reiterate: It's not *just* on our senators and congressmen to get it right on our behalf. It's not *just* on our religious and business leaders. And it's not *just* on our celebrities and pop culture icons. It might start there, in some respects, but it certainly doesn't end there when it comes to clearing our national conscience, because remember, America is run from the bottom up and not the top down. It's on all of us, really, and we ought to get about it.

Understand, we can't seek sweeping change all at once. We won't get anywhere if we keep swinging for the fences and hoping to come up big every time out, because this is one area where it's not about hitting home runs. It's an incremental thing. You'll have to excuse me one final time with these sports metaphors, but it's about stroking a series of seeing-eye singles, and getting a rally going, and chasing the demon pitcher from the game with pluck and perseverance. It's about taking the time to take care.

SPEAK UP!

It's about taking a stand, each and every day, in whatever way possible. I'll toss out a couple of examples from my own life, in hopes of getting us started—and I trust that readers who've stayed with me this long will realize that I do so not to pat myself on the back but to demonstrate how easy it is to lead by making a small stand. (Also, how easy it is to avoid doing so, which I guess is a big part of the problem.) The first incident came to public attention, while the second took place in the relative quiet of a New Hampshire backyard. As it happened, the first incident came during the exploratory phase of my run for president, and on reflection I'm not entirely sure that it paints me in the best light. In fact, it's possible to look on my actions as the rantings of a wild man, but I'll let you readers be the judge. The second incident took place during the campaign itself—and again, I'm afraid I come off as a little too pleased with myself for telling it here. Here, too, you readers will form your own opinion.

The first story: I was in my local video store looking for a movie to watch with my wife, Karen, during one of our few quiet evenings together at home. The clerk in the store recommended *Fargo*, a perversely dark crime story that had played to generally enthusiastic reviews. The movie even earned a Best Actress Oscar for Frances McDormand for her role as a pregnant Midwestern sheriff, and the guy behind the counter at Blockbuster assured me it was a great movie and that I should probably rent it. So I did. Walked right over to that shelf where they had their general titles, grabbed a copy and took it home, and when Karen and I got to the part where they chop up a guy in a grinder we looked at each other and thought, What the heck are we watching here? It was billed as a comedy, but it wasn't funny. It was graphic, and brutal, and completely unnecessary, and it rubbed us in so many wrong ways we had to shut the thing off right there in the middle. For my money, it was little different from a *Texas Chainsaw Massacre*–type snuff movie, and completely unexpected from the movie's packaging and the critical acclaim, and as I pulled the tape from the VCR I became more and more enraged that we had been subjected to it in the first place.

Next morning, I got on the phone to Blockbuster and demanded that they take the movie off their shelves. I was incensed—and on a mission. I was a fairly prominent local customer, so they knew who I was, but I didn't demand any special treatment because I was thinking about running for president at the time. I was personally offended, and it had nothing to do with any kind of political stand. As anonymously as possible, then, I worked my way up from the clerk to the manager, until someone in charge finally threw up his hands and agreed to start doing a better job labeling movies for graphic content—even well-reviewed, Academy Award–winning movies—and I contented myself with this small victory and returned my attention to the rest of my busy life. That is, until I heard from friends whom I had bothered with this tale of frustration that our local Blockbuster hadn't really done all that much in the way of labeling after all, which of course set me off all over again.

I couldn't say firsthand whether the situation had gotten any better, because I had taken my business elsewhere, but from all accounts not much had changed, so I called the store again to remind them of our deal, and it got to where Karen had to tell me to back off because I was driving everyone crazy. I'd made my point, she said, and it was time to move on, so I did, but not before the columnist George Will picked up on the story and wrote about it in the *Washington Post*.

"Pity the fellow who was working at the Blockbuster store when John Kasich spotted a cassette of *Fargo*," the column began, before Will offered his take on whether such an emphatic congressman (a "high-octane, right-to-life Christian") was fit to lead this nation.

The answer, according to Will? Perhaps, perhaps not. "But even assuming there are modern media strategies that could launch a national candidacy from the south wing of the Capitol," Will wrote, "Kasich's presidential plausibility will require someone to turn down the rheostat that controls, if anything does, his expressive energy."

Look, we all have our own gifts, and it's imperative that we use them. I believe I have several, and one of them is to speak out. Usually, I speak out against the status quo on behalf of the little guy, but sometimes I get a little crazy and go off about something like this *Fargo* business, with no real expectation but to let off some steam. I can't imagine it's all that much fun to be on the receiving end of one of my tirades, but I'm here to tell you it isn't much fun to be making the delivery either. I think back to those lonely stands I made on the Budget Committee, or fending off the B-2 bomber, and recognize that there are times when people resent my words, and my actions. But I've always followed my instincts, and my gut, and been true to my values. My purpose has been to influence or sometimes drive the debate, and for the most part I've made a good go of it.

Now, on to the next story. With my presidential campaign in full swing, I traveled to New Hampshire to do some grassroots work, which was about all my campaign could afford. I was scheduled to visit the home of a loyal Republican woman in the Concord area, for one of those coffee-klatch, ladies-auxiliary-type sessions that are essential to this phase of presidential politics. The way it works is the candidate goes from house to house, where all these coffees and teas and meet-and-greets have been set up, and spends a couple hours talking about why he's the greatest guy who ever lived and is therefore deserving of everyone's support. I loved meeting all these new people, even as I hated blowing all that smoke in my own direction, but it was part of the drill. As I would learn soon enough an hour or so before I was due to arrive at this one house the hostess had backed her car out of her own driveway so it would be clear for her guests—and managed to run over the family dog in the process.

Understandably, the woman was all shook up about the death of her dog, and in some way I guess I felt responsible. I raced over to suggest we cancel or at least postpone our session, but she felt she had too many people coming and could not cancel on such short notice. She was crying, and I sat with her and tried to comfort her, but she was determined that the event go off as planned. So it did. It was a little tense, and I caught myself worrying that some other shoe would drop to place everyone else on edge, but the afternoon went off without further incident and as the guests began to leave I stuck around for a bit to see if there was anything I could do to help. I thought the least I could do was to help with the burial. I know the accident wasn't my fault, and that it probably wasn't even my place to be involved at this point, but I felt strongly that I should lend a hand on this. I knew how I would have felt if my dog had just died, so I wanted to help. It was the right thing to do, so I set about it.

By this point, the woman's husband had returned home from work, and the two of us went out back to see about digging a hole. The man struck me as a typical New England Yankee—very practical, and matter-of-fact, with wire-rimmed glasses and a set of suspenders holding up a pair of blue-striped pants—and when I asked him where he wanted to bury the dog he just pointed to the ground at his feet and allowed that this spot was as good as any.

I said, "You can't bury the dog right here. You need shade. It gets hot out here in New Hampshire, in summertime."

He said, "Well, you have a good point."

And so we settled on a spot over by a big tree, and when we

were through with the digging, after we had put the dog in the hole, he began to cover it back up with dirt.

I said, "You can't fill the hole just yet. We haven't said a prayer."

He said, "Well, I guess you're right."

And so he said a few prayers, along the lines of "I hope you catch all the sheep you chase up in heaven." It was a simple sentiment, and yet as I looked over at him I could see tears rolling down his cheeks. As moments go, it was moving, and after we filled in the hole he looked like he was ready to go back inside.

I said, "We're not quite through. We don't have a marker."

The husband said, "You're right." And then he disappeared into the garage and returned with a nice stone to mark the grave, and when we had finally done a respectful job of it I thanked the woman for her courage and hospitality and made to leave. Trouble was, at just that moment, I noticed a reporter still in the house. He'd been covering the campaign, and apparently he'd picked up on something and hung back to see what this extra matter was.

On a personal level, I couldn't abide that this was now open for public inspection, and I said as much. I walked straight over to the reporter and said, "This is a private moment here. I'm trusting you not to write about this, or to share it with anyone else. It's hard enough on these good people to lose their dog like this, without having to read about it in the papers."

I wasn't as emphatic as I might have been over that Blockbuster incident, because of course I had a campaign to run and it would not do to come across as any kind of loose cannon, but I was firm. My "expressive energy" was everywhere apparent. And, sure enough, the story never made the papers—although after a while it did start making the rounds. A couple weeks later, I got a call from my campaign office, indicating that our hostess had spoken out on the subject, and it seemed I had become known (among her circle of friends, at least), as "that man who helped to bury my dog."

I mention this story because that's what it's like to run for president—and it's also what it's like to do the right thing by each other. And that's what it's like to lead—in big ways and small, it's much the same. I hope readers realize by now that I hate telling stories like these on myself, because I don't want to come across as some blowhard, but I do so because they carry an important message: Even such a small kindness as helping to bury someone's dog can go a long way toward setting America right once again.

I'm smiling as I write this, because whenever I catch myself kicking up some dust on some new issue that has set me reeling, or ripping into some poor, unsuspecting soul like that Blockbuster clerk, I catch myself thinking, Here I go again. Or, Why me? And then I think, Well, why not me? Remember, it's on each of us, to do what we can, and for good or ill this is what I do. Standing alone is never easy, but if your words create an impact you can build a team for positive change.

But that's me. What about you?

If you're a doctor, do you make house calls in the middle of the night when you're bone tired and looking to 7:00 A.M. rounds at the hospital the next morning?

If you're an airline ticketing agent, do you stay late to book reservations for a family after their 11:00 P.M. flight is suddenly canceled?

If you're a teacher, do you plead for parental involvement, and go out of your way to call on parents at home?

If you're a carpenter, donating your services to Habitat for Humanity, will you give up another few weekends to build another house, beyond your initial commitment?

Will you call your boss on his or her behavior that might have been out of line?

Will you let bygones be bygones and forget an old feud?

Will you provide health care for your employees, even if you think that doing so will wreak havoc on your budget?

Make no mistake: It's all a virus, and we pass it on. We can either pass on the good virus, or we can pass on the bad one, and this is where our legacies are built. Our parents did it for us, and now it's on us to do the same for our children, to do our part to build a world they can be proud to inherit. Just like baseball players and politicians and famous entertainers are only remembered in a snapshot, that's how the rest of us are remembered as well, and now that I'm finally a father myself I've begun to watchdog myself in this area, to redouble my efforts to make good and lasting decisions, which might in turn lead to a good and lasting impression.

THE POWER TO LEAD

It's the little things, the seeing-eye singles, that will take us where we want to go. We make great strides with small steps. Do I get it right, each and every time out of the gate? Not even close. I'm endlessly frustrated that I don't do enough with my time on this earth. That I sometimes fail. That I feel envy, and jealousy, and all those negative emotions. That I can't always find the time to be fully in the moment with my daughters. That I'm not always so quick to grant someone the benefit of the doubt, and sometimes a little too quick to judge. But then I catch myself and realize it's like I'm still a little kid, back in McKees Rocks, playing ball. I fall down, and I get dirty, but I get right back up and dust myself off and mean to do a better job of it the next time.

That's the bottom line of it right there, the meaning to do a better job of it the next time, because that covers just about everything. Honesty. Integrity. Personal responsibility. Faith. Humility. Accountability. All those good things I wrote about earlier . . . they're all tied together, don't you think? And they all reach back to the values that shaped us as children—values that whether we care to admit it continue to shape our communities and our future.

Be mindful. Be vigilant. Demand better—of one another, and of ourselves. These are our marching orders. Go ahead and tell the guy at the video store to do a better job labeling his titles so people can have some idea what they're taking home . . .

Go ahead and lend a hand to your neighbor in distress—or even to a stranger whose path you just happened to cross . . .

Go ahead and tell your kid you won't buy him that Randy Moss jersey, because Randy Moss represents everything that's crass and off-putting about professional sports . . .

Go ahead and turn off MTV when *The Osbournes* comes on, and refuse to celebrate the drug-filled lifestyle it depicts . . .

Go ahead and talk about an outrage or an injustice over the water cooler at work, because if we're afraid to call attention to the elephant in the room the elephant will hold sway . . .

Go ahead and share your gifts with the world around you, even if those gifts have nothing to do with what you do for a living . . .

Go ahead and do what you can, where you can, whenever you can—because that's leadership, and it's in the doing, the taking care.

Case in point: I have a friend who has "adopted" a lonely old man he chanced upon a couple years back. The poor guy has bad teeth, and so my friend takes him to the dentist, and makes sure he follows through on his treatment, and even picks up a bill now and then. Why? Because he can, I guess. And because he must.

Another case in point: There's a teacher in another friend's school district who arrives at her desk every single morning an hour and a half before the morning bell, a full hour earlier than she's meant to arrive according to her teacher's union contract. Why? Because she's found over the years that kids are more likely to reach out to her for extra help—with school or with anything else—if they don't have to schedule an appointment to do so, and that it's a liberating thing for students to know she is always there. Also, because she can, because she must.

People ask me all the time, if I feel so strongly about these societal issues, why I don't consider returning to politics. But I maintain that politics is not the only arena where change happens, or where values count. I left it all on the field when I retired from Congress. Is there a chance I'd go back? Of course there is, but right now I'm trying to figure out what I can do in the world where I live. I don't need to be in politics to bring about change. I don't need to be in the public eye. In the private sector, I can work quietly to ensure that these values are at least upheld in my corner of the business world. And let's not lose sight of the fact that my father was a mailman. My grandparents hardly spoke any English. They could never have conceived of me writing a book, sounding an all-important message that might resonate across this land. And yet here I am, putting the final touches to just such a book—speaking out, yet again!—and if I can do it, you can, too.

Somebody is always watching. It's bigger than the mommy-cam and daddy-cam notions I've been kicking around in these pages. It's a people-cam, and there's one mounted in every room, on every corner, and atop every building, and last I checked there's no off button. If you're a boss, the people who work for you are watching you at every turn. They're looking on at how you treat your employees, how you accommodate their family emergencies and financial hardships, how you reward their loy-alty. If you're a doctor, your patients know what it means to be in your care. If you're a veteran athlete, your younger teammates are looking down to see what you're doing at your locker, and look-ing to carry themselves in some version of the same way. If you're a teacher, your colleagues are looking to follow your lead, just as your students are taking cues from how you conduct yourself in moments of stress or conflict. And if you're a parent, your chil-dren are watching. At all times.

Everyone is a leader to someone else. Remember it, and do your part, and know that when your time is up you'll have made a contribution on the strength of your leadership. I'm like every-one else when it comes to building a legacy. I want to be re-membered for the good that I've done, and not so much for the mistakes I made along the way. I want to know that when it comes time to sit through the movie of my life, in that big mul-tiplex in the sky, I'll be able to answer for my actions. I'll be sit-ting there, with the Big Guy right next to me, a jumbo tub of popcorn between us and a bottled water fitted into the cup holder in the seat back in front of me, and I'd just as soon have it be a pleasant viewing experience as not. Really, if I'm up there with Him, I don't want to have to be looking away from the screen three-quarters of the way through the movie of my life, and so I aim to get it right. Can we get it right each and every time? Absolutely not. We're not perfect. But we can aim to try.

This last is the bottom line, wouldn't you agree? Make the effort. Be counted. Believe in a greater good. Act. Think in the back of your mind about the footprints you want to leave behind, and then set about making them, because let's face it, the way we live and the choices we make add up to our shared legacy. Stand for something, and those footprints will take care of themselves.

INDEX

INDEX

INDEX

INDEX